ephesians

A 90-Day Devotional
on the Book of Ephesians

By Dr. Deborah Waterbury

First Printing by Love Everlasting Ministries in 2016

Second Printing by DebWaterbury, Inc. 4/21/2017

ISBN-13: 978-0998920856

ISBN-10: 0998920851

BISAC: Religion / Biblical Studies / Paul's Letters

Library of Congress Control Number: 2017905975

Printed in the United States of America

Introduction

One of the most rewarding ways to study the bible is expositionally. Whereas reading through God's Word for content and personal meaning has great impact within the life of the believer, breaking the verses apart and digging deeper for context and language will bring enlightenment beyond simple reading.

Additionally, daily devotional time is paramount for every Christian. All of us need some amount of time with our Father every day, and daily devotion guides are an excellent tool in this endeavor. There are so many wonderful devotionals on the market today that none of us has an excuse for not having that personal time every day.

It is with these two thoughts in mind that I developed my series for daily devotionals. Each book, in this case the book of Ephesians, is broken up into a short expositional devotion taken verse by verse so that the reader is actually doing a complete study of the book while she spends needed time with her Father each day. Each devotion is designed so that it can be completed in fifteen minutes or less with everything the reader needs right here in this book to have her daily personal time.

Each day begins with the verse(s) consecutively written out, followed by a short exposition and application. Next the reader will have a "Study/Meditation" question for further contemplation, which is followed by a short optional prayer. Once the reader has completed this short daily devotion guide, she will have done a complete expositional study of the book.

It will always be my contention that our lives are fully incomplete as believers unless we know our Father and Savior better. What better way is there to do that than to study His Holy Word more indepth? I realize that many of the reasons some of us have for not having a personal quiet time with God is no time and no idea of what to do. These devotions are short, complete, and allow deep study without a lot of preparation or too much time.

I pray that since you've picked this book up long enough to read the Introduction that you will also dedicate that fifteen minutes each day to your Lord. I promise you that only peace and joy come from spending time with Him. I promise you that He is there. I promise you that it will not be time ill spent, and I promise you that study of God's Word will only bring deeper communion with Him and exceedingly more understanding of who He is.

God bless you.

Grace and Peace

Ephesians 1:1-2

"Paul, an apostle of Christ Jesus, by the will of God. To the saints who are in Ephesus, and are faithful in Christ. Grace to you and peace from God our Father and the Lord Jesus Christ."

Paul generally greets his readers with very similar words in all of his letters, and often we breeze right by them, much like we would a "Dear Jane" in a letter of today. However, Paul prays the two things for his readers that hit at the very heart of the Gospel: grace and peace. It is only by God's unmerited and all-encompassing grace that any of us have this gift of salvation. It is certainly not by anything we did, nor is it maintained by anything we will do. We will live in eternity with our Father and Savior simply because of God's grace.

And then once that grace has been bestowed on us, only then do we have true peace, the peace that surpasses all understanding. That peace comes from the realization that this earthly life is only a shadow of the things to come and we have forever to enjoy forever! Paul prays grace and peace on his readers because they have been given the one so that they may live in the other. Because we, as believers, belong to this same group of saints, we have the same privileges to these two gifts. That's the Gospel and it's magnificent!

– Study/Meditation –

Do you live every day in light of the grace you've been given and the peace which should follow it? In what ways could you better realize them today?
(For further study on grace, read John 1)

Father, thank You for giving me a grace undeserved and for the peace that I share with all believers because of it. You are generous and loving and mighty, and I worship You in that today and all of my life. Amen.

1

Heaven Forever!!

Ephesians 1:3

"Blessed be the God and Father of our Lord Jesus Christ, who has blessed us in Christ with every spiritual blessing in the heavenly places."

That phrase "in the heavenly places" is used in two other instances in Ephesians, once in reference to Jesus being seated "in the heavenly places" (1:22) and then to believers who will be raised up to be with Jesus "in the heavenly places."(2:6) Here Paul is blessing God because of what we receive as a result of Christ's sacrifice, which are blessings in the heavenly places.

Do not let the significance of this phrase and proclamation slip by you, for in it we get our eternal perspective as opposed to this temporal one. We have been promised rewards and blessings that extend far beyond getting what we think are blessings in this fallen world. We have been promised blessings in heavenly places, eternal places. We won't simply wake up one day in heaven and exist there; we will live eternally there under the very blessings of God. We will live eternally there under a privileged existence....in heaven!

For that, fellow believers, we should praise and magnify and bless the name of Jesus every single day.

– Study/Meditation –

What do you think it means to "bless God"? How can we do that daily?

Father, thank You for sending Your blessed Son, Jesus Christ, to secure for me these eternal rewards in heaven. I praise and magnify Your Name and I love You. Amen

In Him Before the Foundation of Time

Ephesians 1:4

"Even as he chose us in him before the foundation of the world that we should be holy and blameless before him."

What a glorious passage is Ephesians 1:4! First of all, God chose us, each one of us individually, in Christ. That means He determined that those of us who are in Christ would be in Christ long before we made the decision to follow Him. Now, I understand that sounds somewhat like a paradox, and some would argue that He simply chose that there would be a group who would believe. However, this passage clearly states that before my decision was made to receive Christ as my Savior, a decision that was indeed a necessary step in my salvation, God determined that I would do this. He chose me! I find that so tremendously beautiful. And as if that weren't enough, Paul goes on to remind us that this choice was made "before the foundation of the world." Before the first moment of Genesis 1 occurred, God placed His mighty finger on me and determined me to be His. It had absolutely nothing to do with something I did at that point, since I didn't exist. God chose His children.

To be sure, this has caused major controversy in the church today. It is quite simple to determine why. When I acquiesce to the fact that it was God who chose first so that I might then do so, I am not the instigator, and therefore the control has been taken from me. Human nature is completely adverse to not having at least some measure of control. However, God is either God in complete sovereignty or He can't be God at all. As R.C. Sproul once said, if God isn't in control of every molecule everywhere, then there is a possibility that one little molecule out of His control could land somewhere and change the course of history, in which case, He would no longer be God. Instead of arguing, let us look to Him for wisdom and discernment in this area, gleaning our knowledge from His Word. And then let us rejoice in the fact that we do, indeed, serve a God who is truly God.

(continued)

– Study/Meditation –

Meditate on God being God today. What must it look like for Him to truly be God? (*For further study, read 1 Corinthians 1:27-30 and Romans 9*)

*Father, help me to lay aside my own humanness so that I can
see and worship Your God-ness. I praise You today in Your
sovereignty and I thank You for choosing one such
as me. Amen.*

Ephesians 1:5-6

"(In love) he predestined us for adoption through Jesus Christ, according to the purpose of his will, to the praise of his glorious grace, with which he has blessed us in the Beloved."

Paul continues to praise God in these two verses for the glorious "why" of our salvation and one aspect of the "how". However, first and foremost, he is praising God for our adoption into this heavenly family. We did not belong. We have no reason in and of ourselves to belong, but God in His love chose to bring us in. And once that adoption took place through Jesus Christ, it was final. We are now called the Children of God (Romans 9:25-26).

In this part of the phrase, we are given the first aspect of the "how" of our salvation – in His love. Because of God's great love, we have been adopted into the family (Ephesians 2:4-5). This is glorious enough, but the "why" is equally so.

We were adopted into the family of God "to the praise of His glorious grace." We were adopted, not because of something we did or even would do; we were adopted in order to show God's amazing grace. We were given a home in Glory so that the grace and mercy of God might be manifested for all to see. It is never about us. It's always about God. His great love is that He has allowed us to see that and to live in it. God's love is displayed in that He chose to adopt unworthy sinners into His Kingdom so that they would see His amazing grace. That, my friends, is worth singing about.

– Study/Meditation –

How does the act of salvation show the glory of God? Why is it so important to understand that it is never about us?

Father, thank You for showing me Your love in showing me Your mercy and grace. Help me to manifest only You in my life so that others might also see You in that glory. Amen.

5

The Excesses of Grace

Ephesians 1:7-8

"In him we have redemption through his blood, the forgiveness of our trespasses, according to the riches of his grace, which he lavished upon us, in all wisdom and insight."

That word "redemption" can be one we are so familiar with as believers that we gloss over it as we read. However, to be redeemed, thus having received redemption, means that our rights and privileges and freedoms which we otherwise had lost were purchased for us. We have no rights to heaven or any of the blessings God gives, but in His mercy, God sent His Son, the Beloved, to come to this earth to purchase those rights for us by dying on the cross in payment for our sins. In short, we have redemption through the blood of Jesus Christ.

Paul also says in these verses that this redemption is for the forgiveness of our trespasses "according to the riches of his grace, which he lavished upon us." Probably one of the hardest things for some of us to do is to really accept, beyond a shadow of a doubt, that we have been forgiven of our sins. We look into the mirror and see all that we are, and the reality of that sinful creature can make us doubt God's forgiveness. But Paul reminds us that it was given because of God's grace, not our actions, and that grace was actually lavished on us. It was given so completely that it literally covers us with excesses of grace!

What a loving and awesome God we serve!

– Study/Meditation –

What does the word "lavish" mean to you? How does that translate into how God pours His grace out on you?

Father, Your grace is something I cannot understand, but I receive it and praise You for it. Thank You for loving me so completely and lavishly. Amen.

The Mystery of God

Ephesians 1:9-10

"...making known to us the mystery of his will, according to his purpose, which he set forth in Christ as a plan for the fullness of time, to unite all things in him, things in heaven and things on earth."

Paul tells us in Romans 1 that no man can say he doesn't see the Hand of God nor can any man truly deny that He exists. However, God has chosen only to reveal the mystery of His will, that is salvation through Jesus Christ, to His children. That in and of itself is reason for us to be joyful and thankful that we have been given this glimpse into the mystery of His will. However, very often we wonder at God's timing, don't we? Why did He wait until Adam and Eve sinned? Why did thousands of years have to go by before He sent His Son to save the earth? Why hasn't His Son returned? Why has my life gone the way it has?

The questions can go on and on, and often they do. We question His timing all of the time. Yet Paul tells us in Ephesians that God has given us a glimpse into the mystery of His will which will perfectly be orchestrated in the "fullness of time." Part of our enduring faith in our Father is trusting that He has it all under control. His "fullness of time" is, indeed, full and perfect, as is His plan. We trust that and are grateful and thankful that we have been given a glimpse, a glimpse that gave us Jesus and eternity. Amen.

– Study/Meditation –

Why do you think so many do not see the truth of Jesus Christ, which Paul describes as the mystery of God's will?
(For further study, read 1 Corinthians 1:18-31)

Father, help me to live correctly in the truths You have given me while I continually seek to know You more. You have revealed much of Yourself in Your Word and I will place my heart and thoughts there. Thank You for giving of Yourself in Your Word and for allowing me to see a glimpse into Your plan. Amen.

The Inheritance of the Saints

Ephesians 1:11-12

have obtained an inheritance, having been predestined according to the purpose of him who works all things according to the counsel of his will. We who first hoped in Christ have been destined and appointed to live for the praise of his glory"

Very few people on this earth are fortunate enough to get something significant and give nothing in return. Generally we work hard for what we get, and often the amount of work we render is not quite equal to the return we receive. However, in God's economy, we receive the glorious riches of His Kingdom – an inheritance – without having done anything at all for it. We have received this inheritance in Christ and only because of His work and sacrifice. We know this has been freely given to us because God's Word makes it clear: Our Lord decided to give this inheritance to us each individually before we were even born. We were predestined to receive it, and all of this is because of Christ's work and God's will. Paul makes a sweeping statement in this verse about God's sovereignty, not only over our eternal reward but also in relation to "all things." Paul said that God "works all things according to the counsel of his will."

Furthermore, we know that both clarity and security are wonderful things. It is in our human natures to want clear purpose in the things we do and then to feel secure that those things are not for naught. God gives us both of those things.

First, the purpose and appointment for our lives has been given in God's Word many times, and Paul reminds us again of it here. We have a destiny and a purpose to live for the praise of the glory of God. That means that every single thing we do while on this earth should be done with God not only in mind, but central. All that we do is to be about Him and demonstrating for a dying world His magnificent glory. That old saying, "What would Jesus do," is appropriate for all of our lives.

However, even more appropriate would be, "What would show how glorious God is?" Let us measure every action and reaction in our lives by one measuring rod: God's glory. Let us seek in all ways to show a world that is dying without Him how truly awesome and glorious He is.

– Study/Meditation –

What do you think it means to "bless God"? How can we do that daily?

Father, thank You for sending Your blessed Son, Jesus Christ, to secure for me these eternal rewards in heaven. I praise and magnify Your Name and I love You. Amen

Sealed with the Holy Spirit

Ephesians 1:13-14

"In him you also, when you heard the word of truth, the gospel of your salvation, and believed in him, were sealed with the promised Holy Spirit, who is the guarantee of our inheritance until we acquire possession of it, to the praise of his glory."

Broken promises are unfortunately a fact of life in the midst of fallen humanity. Promises are made and kept, but they are also made and broken. That is simply not the case with God, and Paul reminds us of how God has given us security in His promises when we receive the Holy Spirit. In Luke 24:49, Jesus promised his disciples that they would not be left alone when He left this earth, but that the Holy Spirit would descend upon them from on high. This happened on the Day of Pentecost as recorded in Acts 2. Consequently, all of us who have believed on Jesus Christ as Savior receive this security through the seal of the Holy Spirit.

The word "seal" is used in three other ways in the New Testament: a "seal" was used as a secure closure for something, as with Christ's tomb in Matthew 27:66; a "seal" was used to describe a sign of authenticity as with Abraham's circumcision being called a "seal of his righteousness" in Romans 4:11; and a "seal" was used to describe the mark God places on the foreheads of His children in Revelation 7:3 as a sign of protection. However we think the word "seal" should be applied to us in terms of the Holy Spirit, we know that He has been given to us as an authentic sign of safety and security in God's love. In other words, God's promises are always fulfilled; the seal of the Holy Spirit is another manifestation of that fact.

God doesn't leave us floundering here on earth until He comes again. He has given us a clear purpose, as we studied yesterday from verse twelve, and a wonderful seal of security so that we can know beyond a shadow of a doubt that His love for us is real and constant. He is a loving and devoted Father who cares for His children.

– Study/Meditation –

How does the presence of the Holy Spirit within you give you security about God and His promises? What is the purpose of the Holy Spirit besides being a demonstration of security? (*For further study on the Holy Spirit, read Acts 2.*)

Father, thank You for sending the Comforter, the Holy Spirit, to both guide and direct me through Your words while also giving me a sure proof of Your love for me. Amen.

9

Pray in Good Times and Bad

Ephesians 1:15-16

"For this reason, because I have heard of your faith in the Lord Jesus and your love toward all the saints, I do not cease to give thanks for you, remembering you in my prayers, that the God of our Lord Jesus Christ, the Father of glory, may give you a spirit of wisdom and of revelation in the knowledge of him."

In seasons of doubt and pain when you have difficulty holding firm to your faith, what do you pray for? When you see others in the same sorts of circumstances, what do you pray on their behalf? Paul had just been reminding the church in Ephesus that God had not abandoned them, that He in fact, had left them with the promised Holy Spirit as a security and a guarantee of His protection and promise. His prayer for them in times of trouble, or in times of plenty, was that God would fill them with the knowledge of these great truths. Paul knew, as we should, that circumstances change all of the time, but truth never does.

Our comfort comes in hanging onto those promises and those truths, and that is what we must pray for no matter what is going on around us. Often we pray for our circumstances to change, or we thank God for the good circumstances in our lives. Let us remember to first pray as Paul did, not based on our circumstances but on receiving the abounding and comforting revelations of our Father. Only there will we find the source of the peace that surpasses all understanding.

– Study/Meditation –

What model of prayer do you use most often? How might you alter your prayer life so that you are praying more for revelation and wisdom than for circumstances?

Father, give me the wisdom to see You in all things. Help me to know Your character better and to better listen to the voice of the Holy Spirit as He reveals Your truths to me. Amen.

10

Hearts Enlightened

Ephesians 1:18-20

"Having the eyes of your hearts enlightened, that you may know what is the hope to which he has called you, what are the riches of his glorious inheritance in the saints, and what is the immeasurable greatness of his power toward us who believe, according to the working of his great might that he worked in Christ when he raised him from the dead and seated him at his right hand in the heavenly places."

Paul had begun his prayer for the Ephesians by praying that God would give them a spirit of wisdom and revelation of Him. Notice in these verses that he doesn't simply pray that they receive this knowledge. He uses an interesting phraseology – "having the eyes of your hearts enlighteded." Paul understands that knowledge of God's mercy and grace and power is simply not enough to be His; the demons know this and shudder (James 2:19). Paul's prayer is that they know with their hearts, that they know from their experience. We must know and understand what we have received in God's power and might because we understand the extent of the sin from which we have been forgiven.

As believers, we often miss the magnitude of what God has promised us and what He has already done for us. However, Scripture couldn't be clearer about those things, and rarely is it as clear as it is in this prayer by Paul. He is being even more specific about what it is he wants us to know – God will work in His children those things that are "according to" or "like" those things He worked in Christ Jesus. Did you catch that? God has promised us that He will do for us the same mighty works as He did in His Son! Paul then goes on to enumerate five of those things. We'll look at the first today.

God's great might will be worked in us according to, or like, it was when He raised Jesus from the dead. God has both raised us from the dead spiritually in that He has opened our eyes to sin and conquered our rebellious hearts, and He will raise us up physically. "Death is swallowed up in victory. O death, where is your victory? O death, where is your sting?" (1 Corinthians 15:54-55) This resurrection power is both for now and for eternity, and it has been poured out to us who believe. Let us know our Father, for in that knowing we realize how very much we are loved.

– Study/Meditation –

Think today about who you are and who God is. Of what has He forgiven you? What has He promised you? Can you see Him with the "eyes of your heart"?

Father, thank you for giving me life in the midst of my own depravity. Thank you for the forgiveness You have given me and the promises and hopes that go with that. I love You. Amen.

My Everlasting Bridegroom

Ephesians 1:20-22

"That he worked in Christ when he raised him from the dead and seated him at his right hand in the heavenly places, far above all rule and authority and power and dominion, and above every name that is named, not only in this age but also in the one to come."

We are, by nature, an impatient people. Sometimes we find it difficult to hang our hats on promises because we want to see the results of those promises now. One of the most beautiful things about the promises that Paul is enumerating in Ephesians 1:15-23 is that they are for now. We read yesterday about the resurrection promise, that God raised Christ from the dead and the victory that He gave us over death and sin. The next two promises we see today also come to us as a result of the resurrection of our Lord and Savior, Jesus Christ.

The second promise in this passage is that God has seated Christ at His right hand, giving Him dominion and authority over all things. The "all things" Paul refers to here is truly all things, including Satan and all his minions. Paul said in Colossians 2:15 that at the cross, God disarmed the rulers and authorities and put them to open shame in triumph. That is resurrection power for us now! There is no power over the Bride of Christ except that which comes from Him.

Thirdly, we know that this power is not temporary, but everlasting. The authority of our Savior is for now and forever, and it is complete. We have not been given to a Savior who cannot take care of us, but we belong to a Lord whose power is from now and into forever and is over all things. We truly have nothing to fear from the enemy and his schemes nor from the things of this world. My Everlasting Bridegroom sits on the throne in majesty and might – Hallelujah!!!!

– Study/Meditation –

What do you fear most today? How can you view this fearful
thing in light of Jesus' rule and authority?
(*For further study, read Colossians 1:15-2:15.*)

*Father, thank You for choosing me to belong to Your majestic
Kingdom. Help me to see and know that Your promises in Christ
are for me and that they give me triumph over all evil through
the love of my Savior. Amen.*

Part of the Great Commission

Ephesians 1:22-23

"And he put all things under his feet and gave him as head over all things to the church, which is his body, the fullness of him who fills all in all.

There are two final and glorious things to point out in the last part of this focal passage in Ephesians, but first let's bring some clarity to all of the pronouns in these verses. The pronoun references would read something like this: "And (God) put all things under (Christ's) feet and gave (Christ) as head over all things to the church, which is (Christ's) body, the fullness of (Christ) who fills all in all." Paul has been engaged in a beautiful proclamation of Christ's authority and rule over all that is, all that has been, and all that will be. Then he goes on in summation by reminding his readers that God gave His Son this reign on behalf of His children, the church. God "gave him as head over all things to the church." That is, indeed, glorious!

However, what Paul writes next is equally glorious, and we mustn't miss the magnificence of this final statement. Paul says that Christ's power was given by God over all things to the church "which is his body." That is, the church is the manifestation of Christ's power; it is His body. Consequently, God has chosen to display the beauty and majesty of His Son's glorious power and dominion on this earth through the church. What a privilege and responsibility! Why did Christ give the Great Commission, that the church is to go out into all the world and preach the Gospel to every living creature? Because God's plan has always been that Christ's power and dominion would be manifested by way of His people. Let us with humble gratitude and great sobriety enter into that commission every day; we are the very physical body of Christ on this earth.

What do you think it means to be the "body of Christ"? How does that change or alter the way you might look at your responsibilities while here?

Father, what an awesome and undeserved honor You have given me that I am part of the body of Christ. Help me, Father, to remember both the privilege and responsibility that station represents, and thank You for making me part of it. Amen.

He Occupies Our Lowly Hearts!

Ephesians 2:1-2

"And you were dead in the trespasses and sins in which you once walked, following the course of this world, following the prince of the power of the air, the spirit that is now at work in the sons of disobedience"

Why must we be "born again"? Why isn't there some other manner in which we can become a part of the body of Christ, the very manifestation of His power and dominion here on earth? After he had just written the joyous passage at the end of chapter 1 on Christ's reign and our part in it, Paul gives us the answer to just this question. Why must we be born again? Quite simply, because we were dead. We were absolutely dead, non-living, and therefore we needed new life. Paul could have said that we were lost, which we were, or that we were disillusioned, which was also truly the case. If being lost was the problem, we would need only to be found; if being disillusioned was it, we would need only to be enlightened. However, being lost and disillusioned weren't the causes of our separation from Christ; they were results of that separation.

Have you ever witnessed someone do something unconscionable and think, "How could she do that?" Are you able to look at your own life before Christ and wonder how you could possibly make the choices you made? Paul has just begun explaining our spiritual states before Christ, and in verse 2 of Ephesians 2, he starts to tell us how we were dead in our sins and trespasses. The answer is that before we were given new life in Christ, we were held captive to Satan. We followed after him and the ways of the world. And the horrible thing is that without Christ, without the indwelling power of the Holy Spirit, we had no choice. The only voice we could hear was our own, and that, without the Spirit, is fully guided by the enemy.

How could Paul say we were dead in our trespasses and sins? Because we had no possibility of following Christ, and therefore we had no possibility of eternal life. Yet, in His great love, God entered our hearts and transformed them, giving us life where there was only death, and in that instant the voice of the Savior became real and remarkable and irresistible! The Great God in Heaven came and occupied our lowly hearts!

– Study/Meditation –

How were you dead in your trespasses and sins before accepting
Christ as your Savior? Why did you need to be born again?
(*For further study, read John 3.*)

*Father, thank You for sending Your Son to die for me so that I might
be born again to new life. I honor You with this new life You've given me.
Help me in my endeavors to give it all to You.*

The Remarkable Free Gift of Salvation

Ephesians 2:2b-3

"...the spirit that is now at work in the sons of disobedience – among whom we all once lived in the passions of our flesh, carrying out the desires of the body and the mind, and were by nature children of wrath, like the rest of mankind."

What does it mean to be by nature a child of wrath? Paul has already established that in mankind's state without Christ, it follows Satan, who rules the course of this world. Then Paul goes on to say that we, too, were in that group, as is all of humanity, living according to what we wanted to do or thought about doing. And when reduced down to its basic meaning, if we are defined by what we think and do, then that pretty much sums up our beings. Without Christ, it is our nature to be "anti-Christ;" we are natural "children of wrath," following Satan instead of Jesus.

But from whose wrath are we saved? Paul goes on in Ephesians 5:6 to clear this question up: "Let no one deceive you with empty words, for because of these things the wrath of God comes upon the sons of disobedience." All of mankind, at its nature, is at enmity with God, and because of this, we are all justly under His wrath. It is this fact that makes the free, undeserved gift of salvation all the more remarkable. Without Jesus, we deserve death, and that is precisely what we would receive. However, because of His sacrificial death on the cross, taking all of the penalty for our sins, we have eternal life. This gift is truly remarkable, and even more so is that it is free to all who would receive it. Praise our Father and our Savior, Jesus Christ!!

– Study/Meditation –

Have you ever been the object of condemnation because
of your faith? What, according to the Word, is the reason that those
without Christ simply cannot fathom your faith in Him?
(*Hint: Read 1 Corinthians 2:14; 2 Corinthians 4:3-4; and Matthew 13:19*)

*Father, thank You for coming into my heart and giving me
the ability to see You, for I know that apart from You, I am lost.
Praise be to Your name and Your mercy
forever and ever. Amen.*

15

But God...

Ephesians 2:4-5

"But God, being rich in mercy, because of the great love with which he loved us, even when we were dead in our trespasses, made us alive together with Christ – by grace you have been saved."

There are probably no two more beautiful words in the Bible than the two that begin this passage: "But God." We were lost to our sinful natures, living according to what we wanted and thought. We were by nature children in deserving of the wrath of the Almighty God, wandering around this earth in acquiescence to the powers of Satan. All of this was our state – "But God."

But God, because He is loving and full of mercy, brought us life out of this deadness. But God, though we deserve damnation, gave us this life in Christ. But God, though we could do absolutely nothing to save ourselves, pulled us out of the miry pit of stench and death and because of His grace saved us. None of it is about us. All of it is because of those two words –

But God.

How magnificent that He has intervened on our behalf, so that now it is not only "But God;" it is now also, "With us."

– Study/Meditation –

What does the act of making us alive together with Christ mean?
How should that affect our view of ourselves and of God?

*Father, how awesome is Your grace, O Lord, and how complete is Your mercy!
I praise You and thank You for a love undeserved that is beyond anything
I can truly fathom, a love that brought me life. Amen.*

The Immeasurable Riches of His Grace

Ephesians 2:6-7

"And (God) raised us up with him and seated us with him in the heavenly places in Christ Jesus, so that in the coming ages he might show the immeasurable riches of his grace in kindness toward us in Christ Jesus."

Paul discussed in Ephesians 2:3 that we are, by nature, children of wrath, and we know that because of this, we deserve the judgment of the Almighty God of the Universe. But God, as begun in verse 4, gave us mercy and grace, even in the midst of this wrath-deserving nature, and bestowed on us life. That would certainly be enough and more than we deserve. However, God wasn't finished.

Verse 3 begins with those beautiful words, "But God," and verse 6 begins with a word that is equally astounding – "And." Not only did God lift us up out of death and give us life, He then adds astounding measures to what He has done for us, His children. In the act of raising us to newness of life, He has given us a place in His Kingdom, a place specifically reserved for each of us. Paul can't even find enough superlatives to describe the wonderful things God has done and will do for us. They are immeasurable riches that are given in the very kindness of God according to His grace.

And what is even more astonishing is the time frame: these things are given to us "in the coming ages." We, though deserving of wrath and damnation, have been given indescribable riches and blessings by God that exist in His Kingdom, and receive them forever.

(continued)

The Immeasurable Riches of His Grace – continued

– Study/Meditation –

What is the significance of Paul's words in this passage so far?
Why is it so amazing that God has done these
marvelous things for us?

*Father, I confess to You my sins and shortcomings and I acknowledge
before You that I do not deserve Your love. Yet, I thank You for it,
and I praise You for Your magnificent and awe-inspiring faithfulness
toward me, Your chosen child. Amen.*

17

The Gift of God

Ephesians 2:8-9

*"For by grace you have been saved through faith.
And this is not your own doing; it is the gift of God,
not a result of works, so that no one may boast."*

There is so much that can be said about such a beautiful passage! How do we receive the immeasurable riches of God's grace? We receive them by way of that very same grace! We have to have faith in that grace, in the promises of God and in the saving power of His Son, Jesus Christ. But that faith is not a thing that we do; it's not an independent decision that we make. Faith is a belief that what God said is true, that what Jesus did was real. Faith is the means by which we hang onto the gift that we were given, and that makes it necessary and evident, but it isn't the trigger. God's grace is the trigger; our faith is how we hold onto this grace.

Let us not rearrange Paul's words in an attempt to somehow take any measure of credit for what God has done. God's grace brings our faith and results in His gifts. It's all about His glory and His majesty and the miracles that only He can do. Could that be any more wonderful? Could anything ever be more worthy of our devotion and honor and praise?

– Study/Meditation –

What assurances do we have from these two verses?
How should they offer us freedom and not bondage?

*Father, Your grace is magnificent! I give You all the glory
and honor and praise in the act of my salvation. Amen.*

18

After, Not Before

Ephesians 2:10

"For we are his workmanship, created in Christ Jesus for good works, which God prepared beforehand, that we should walk in them."

Some might find it a little interesting that Paul had just said in verse 9 that our works do not save us, but now in verse 10 he is telling us that these same works are what we were created to do. How can this be? Simply put, our good works come after we are saved, not before. Once God changes our hearts and we accept Christ as our Savior, then we are in a position to do those things that we were created in Christ to do, namely those things that bring glory to our Father. Nothing outside of Christ is good because nothing outside of Him brings Him glory. Therefore it only stands to reason that our "good" works come after we are His. God created us to do these works, He prepared them for us long before, so that our lives would be a testimony to His mercy and grace.

Let us this day and every day walk in those works as a manifestation of the saving grace that allows them in the first place.

– Study/Meditation –

Why is it that one can only do "good" works once she is "in Christ"? What does it mean to you that God prepared the works you are to do "beforehand"? (*For further study, read Psalm 139.*)

Father, give me the wisdom and discernment to know what You have prepared beforehand for me to do. I pray that all of my actions and works bring glory to Your name. Amen.

One Plan and One People

Ephesians 2:11-13

"Therefore remember that at one time you Gentiles in the flesh, called the uncircumcision by what is called the circumcision, which is made in the flesh by hands – remember that you were at that time separated from Christ, alienated from the commonwealth of Israel and strangers to the covenants of promise, having no hope and without God in the world."

The covenant people of God is Israel. God did not institute two separate plans that lead to Him – one for Israel and then one for everyone else. There is one plan and one people, and when we were without God, we were outside of that people. It's important that we remember that. Before God reached down and grafted us into this one people, we were without hope; we were destined for the judgment we rightly deserve. You must remember, as Paul states at the beginning of this passage, from where you came. In so doing, your position becomes all the more precious, and the amazing love of the Father all the more beautiful.

The promise given to the nation of Israel in Genesis 12:3, that God would bless all the children of the world through His covenant with Israel, was as yet unknown to the Gentile nation. Paul's proclamation that they, as believing Christians, were now included in the members of those receiving God's covenant blessings was both glorious and stunning, as it should also be to us. And the only way this became possible, for Jew and Gentile alike, was by way of Jesus Christ, which Paul was careful to point out in this one verse.

First, it is "in Christ" that we are included. It is because of the experience of our spiritual union with Him that we are part of God's family. Second, it is because of

(continued)

"the blood of Christ" that we have been brought near. Only by way of His sacrificial death on the cross was there an avenue for our sins to be dealt with in justice before the Holy God. We have been brought into God's family both in and through our Lord and Savior, Jesus Christ. He is the way, the truth, and the life, and no man comes to the Father except through Him. (John 14:6)

– Study/Meditation –

How do you explain God's plan of salvation? Was it
different for the Jew than it was for the Gentile?
(Hint: Read Romans 10.)

*Father, I honor You in Your holiness and I recognize my own
sinfulness before You. Because of that, Father, I thank You for giving
me a way to Your Kingdom through Your Son, Jesus Christ. You are
holy and righteous and Your mercy endures forever. Amen.*

20

The Peace of Christ

Ephesians 2:14-16

"For he himself is our peace, who made us both one and has broken down in his flesh the dividing wall of hostility by abolishing the law of commandments and ordinances, that he might create in himself one new man in place of the two, so making peace, and might reconcile us both to God in one body through the cross, thereby killing the hostility."

Ethnic tensions between Jews and non-Jews continue to this day, and certainly that was never God's intention. God did not establish two separate plans to Him – one for Jews and one for everyone else. On the contrary, Jesus was always the plan and His sacrifice for all people, Jew and Gentile alike, was God's intention from the foundation of time.

As Paul states here, Jesus is the peace between the nations, referring to the temple wall, or the "wall of hostility," that divided them before Jesus' one final and perfect sacrifice was made on the cross. This one sacrifice created one people, a people who could all equally receive salvation, and we can be sure that this salvation was never available before Him. Since perfection has always been the standard, then only a perfect sacrifice would bring salvation. Jesus was and is the means by which that standard is met – one people with one God and one Savior bringing peace. That is and always has been God's plan, and our thanksgiving should be in that we are part of it.

For that, fellow believers, we should praise and magnify and bless the name of Jesus every single day.

(continued)

20

The Peace of Christ — *continued*

– Study/Meditation –

Why do you think racial and ethnic tensions still exist today, in spite of everything the Bible teaches us? What is the answer to this tension? (*Read Colossians 3:11-17.*)

Father, help us to see each other in terms of Christ. Only in You do we have the ability to love each other correctly. Please give me that love that brings peace. Amen.

21

The Access of the Children

Ephesians 2:17-18

"And he came and preached peace to you who were far off and peace to those who were near. For through him we both have access in one Spirit to the Father."

One of the things that angered many Jewish leaders about Jesus was that He wasn't a separatist. He dined in the houses of sinners and tax collectors. He allowed women of ill repute to sit at his feet and wash his feet with their hair. He healed on the Sabbath. However, He still made no bones about the fact that He was Jewish; He certainly never tried to deny His lineage. What Jesus did come to do was save. He came to fulfill God's purpose of creating for Himself a people who would be separate unto Him, not separate unto themselves, and this ultimately had nothing to do with earthly heritage.

Paul wrote in Galatians 3:28, "There is neither Jew nor Greek, there is neither slave nor free, there is neither male nor female, for you are all one in Christ Jesus." God's children are one in His Son, and only there exists the peace that surpasses all understanding, only there do we receive the blessing of the indwelling Holy Spirit, and only there are we set free.

– Study/Meditation –

What does it mean to you to be a member of God's family?

*Father, You are glorious and merciful in the peace
You brought to us in Christ. Help me to live in that peace while
living as a member of Your family. Amen.*

33

Citizens of the Household of God

Ephesians 2:19-20a

"So then you are no longer strangers and aliens, but you are fellow citizens with the saints and members of the household of God, built on the foundation of the apostles and prophets."

Citizenship holds certain rights, as well as certain responsibilities. The same is true as citizens of God's Kingdom. Once outside of this station, now we claim the inheritance promised its citizens, namely eternity in heaven forever in the presence of the Almighty God. Likewise, there are also responsibilities to this citizenship. When we behave contrary to the laws and regulations established by our King, we pay the consequences. As with any loving and kind ruler, God knows what will bring us joy and what will inevitably bring us sorrow. When we do not uphold the laws of God's land, then as citizens of that land we are forfeiting the joy due its members. Instead, we are reducing ourselves to being citizens of the world, receiving all of the things we were so fortunate to leave behind.

Let us remember our citizenship, a citizenship bought for us by the precious blood of Jesus Christ, and live as that kind of people with all of the privileges and joy that come with it.

– Study/Meditation –

How does neglecting our gift of citizenship into God's
Kingdom ultimately bring us sorrow? How can you improve in this
area starting today?

Father, thank You for giving me citizenship into Your Kingdom,
mercifully taking me out of the world and into Your loving arms.
Help me to remember how to conduct myself as a
citizen of Heaven. Amen.

The Cornerstone

Ephesians 2:20b-22

"Christ Jesus being the cornerstone, in whom the whole structure, being joined together, grows into a holy temple in the Lord. In him you also are being built together into a dwelling place for God by the Spirit."

The cornerstone in a structure is the largest stone laid when the structure is being built. It has to be accurate and perfectly laid so that every other stone in the building fits perfectly into it. It is the stone to which every other stone is adapted. That is Jesus for us. The structure of the church is laid with Jesus as its cornerstone, its Chief Stone, and because of that, each of us fits together perfectly in His Kingdom. Every member of the Kingdom of Christ is joined together by way of Christ; therefore, the resulting structure, or the Church, grows into a holy temple, the perfect habitation for the Holy Spirit. That temple is then represented in the church, as a whole, and also in each individual member. We are being built into a holy temple because the perfect Lamb of God is our Cornerstone.

With that in mind, one would think that for the church, the body of believers, unity would come naturally. However, in a world where "independence" is stressed above just about anything else, unity is an issue and it can be an issue for the church, too. Apparently this wasn't a new issue as Paul has been speaking on it for many verses. Consequently, it is no surprise that he ends these thoughts on unity by reminding the Ephesians, and us, that we are being built together into a dwelling place for our Lord. Each of us is a different, unique part of the body, but each of us fits together with the other pieces to perfectly form a temple for the presence of God in the Holy Spirit. There is truly no place for disunity among parts of a whole because the result is a structure without stability. More than any other group, the church must strive for peace and harmony among its members; it represents the Holy God to a dying world, a world of loose foundations and shifting sands.

(continued)

The Cornerstone – *continued*

– Study/Meditation –

What does it mean in your everyday life to be built as part
of the temple inhabiting the Holy Spirit?
(*For further study, read 1 Peter 2:1-12.*)

*Father, help me to be mindful of who I am in Christ
and of what my body and my actions represent. Keep me ever
conscious of being the very temple of the Spirit. Amen.*

Our Help in Present Struggle

Ephesians 3:1-3

"For this reason I, Paul, a prisoner for Christ Jesus on behalf of you Gentiles – assuming that you have heard of the stewardship of God's grace that was given to me for you, how the mystery was made known to me by revelation, as I have written briefly."

Paul had just been encouraging the believers in Ephesus about their inheritance and citizenship in the Kingdom of God and how they should be unified as a body because of this common gift. However, Paul is writing this letter while in Nero's prison, so he also realizes the need to continue encouraging them given his current circumstances.

It is so difficult at times to be encouraged in the midst of trials. Sometimes it can feel like we're sinking in a pit of mire so thick that there is no possible way to even see the top, much less swim to it. Yet, the truth is that if anyone had reason to feel himself covered in miles and miles of mire, it was the Apostle Paul. But he had a secret that allowed him to stop the sinking, and it was this secret he shared in these first few verses of chapter 3. In verses 2 and 3 he reminds the Ephesians of how God has graciously used him and had even revealed to him the mysteries of the Gospel, even though he was, in his own words, the worst of sinners. Paul's trick was to remember the amazing things God had done in his life, using those things as a sort of anchor that held him up in the mire of disappointment and tragedy.

God is faithful to His children, and Paul knew that; God had proven that over and over to him. He has proven Himself to us, too, just as He had to the Ephesians. When you're sinking in the mire of your circumstances, hang onto the memories of God's unfailing faithfulness to you. Hang onto the fact that He lifted you out of

(continued)

Our Help in Present Struggle – continue

eternal mire into the glory of heaven, even in the midst of your sin. Do what Paul did and recount all that God has given; the mire will soon appear as inconsequential to eternity as it really is.

– Study/Meditation –

What has God brought you out of in life? How should remembering these things encourage you today?

Father, thank You for Your faithfulness. Thank You for bringing me out of the depth of my sin into Your eternal presence. Help me to remember all that You have done for me in my times of despair and weakness while on this earth. Amen.

God's Mysteries

Ephesians 3:4-5

"When you read this, you can perceive my insight into the mystery of Christ, which was not made known to the sons of men in other generations as it has now been revealed to his holy apostles and prophets by the Spirit."

Everyone loves a good mystery. It's somewhat fun to try to figure out the end or what someone is trying to keep from you. The mystery of Christ was not designed that way, nor was it designed the way other "mystery religions" of that time period were. Other mystery religions were designed so that only a select few individuals could know the truth of the mystery, and they remained exclusive within the community in that knowledge. The mystery of Christ, however, was always to be revealed to God's children, and Paul is reminding the Ephesians of this fact.

The mystery of Christ is revealed by way of His apostles and prophets who wrote the words given them by the Spirit – the Bible. These words are there for all of God's children to read and learn and digest. God has kept nothing from us, and that is just one more way He shows how intimate and complete is His love for us. Read His Word today. The mysteries of all life and happiness are contained within.

– Study/Meditation –

How should we view the privilege we have of being able to read the Word of God any time we want? In light of that, what is the correct view of God's Word?

Father, in Your love You have given us the answer to the mystery of Christ, which is available to any who will read it. Thank You for that love and direction for our lives while here on this earth. Amen.

Fellow Heirs

Ephesians 3:6

"This mystery is that the Gentiles are fellow heirs, members of the same body, and partakers of the promise in Christ Jesus through the gospel."

It must have been very mysterious to the Jewish nation in Paul's day to hear that Gentiles could now receive the same eternal benefits as Israel through the saving blood of Jesus Christ. The Apostle Paul proclaims in this verse that the inheritance of God's eternal riches, being a member of His holy Family, and receiving all of the promises from Christ is now available to all peoples from all nations "through the gospel." Those last three words really were the mystery.

You see, the Jews would have been very familiar with the Old Testament prophesies given to Abraham and Isaiah and expressed by the psalmists that many from the Gentile nation would be brought into the fold – but into the Jewish fold. They expected the other nations to become Jews, to take on their ceremonial laws and customs. The real mystery they were hearing was that those laws and regulations had been fulfilled in Jesus Christ and that His sacrifice was then available to any person, Jew or Greek. This is the truest meaning of what Paul said in Galatians 3:28, "There is neither Jew nor Greek, there is neither slave nor free, there is neither male nor female, for you are all one in Christ Jesus." There are not two paths to eternity – one for the Jew and one for everyone else – but one path, our Lord Jesus Christ. This mystery has been revealed and it is glorious therein.

– Study/Meditation –

What does it mean to be joint heirs, members of the same body, and partakers of the promises of Christ? How can a true understanding of this "mystery" bring peace and joy to God's children?

Father, thank You for the saving blood of Your Son, Jesus Christ, and all that His sacrifice has offered us. Help me to live a life that is being sanctified daily in light of what was done for me on the cross. Amen.

The Beauty of God's Control

Ephesians 3:7

*"Of this gospel I was made a minister according
to the gift of God's grace, which was given me
by the working of his power."*

Mankind is a very "me-centered" species; we tend to be the focal point of our own existences. This is who we are at our very cores. I see everything through a lens that begins with me, just as you see everything from a lens that begins with you. Given that one fact, it's a difficult thing not to translate all of life as if each of us was at the center.

In Paul's prayer of encouragement for the Ephesians, however, he demonstrates what it looks like to have a "God-centered" view of reality as opposed to a "me-centered" one. He says that his ministering to them the Gospel of Jesus Christ was "according to the gift of God's grace" and that it was given to him "by the working of his (God's) power." Paul had long before lain down anything of himself in favor of reality, which is that God is truly in control of all things. The apostle is giving encouragement, and this encouragement is based on the one and only thing that can give us peace in this world: God is the giver of all things and the author of everything that occurs in our lives. Let us be greatly encouraged today in the midst of whatever happens to us that our Father is sovereignly in control of all of it.

– Study/Meditation –

What encouragement can you take from the fact that
God is truly in control of your life today?

*Father, I thank You that my life is in Your hands.
Help me to rest in that wonderful knowledge. Amen.*

Even the Least of Us

Ephesians 3:8-9

"To me, though I am the very least of all the saints, this grace was given, to preach to the Gentiles the unsearchable riches of Christ, and to bring to light for everyone what is the plan of the mystery hidden for ages in God who created all things."

There are truly moments when we look into the mirror of God's grace and think, "Why me?" Most certainly we should occasionally wonder such things. Why does God choose to use the most unlikely of humanity to do His will? Paul wondered at this and equally marveled at the fact that he was used so significantly to spread the Gospel of Christ.

In his letter of encouragement to the Ephesians, he continues in this vein in verses 8-9 by pointing out how beautiful it is that God had chosen to use him, "the least of all the saints," to preach the Good News to them, revealing truths as yet revealed in ages past. Paul is saying, "Be encouraged, my dear friends. God is weaving a tapestry that is marvelous and intricate and purposeful, and He has chosen even men such as me to be His tools in this work. Be encouraged that our Lord, full of mercy and grace, is revealing His plan to us."

When life throws us into a loop and we can't seem to see the end, we must remember and be encouraged that God is the Weaver and Creator of this tapestry and that He is doing all of it according to His plan. And even more wonderful is that He has chosen us, even though oftentimes we would never do the same in His shoes. That is an encouragement no matter what is happening.

– Study/Meditation –

What sorts of things make you feel unworthy of service in
God's Kingdom? What do you think God would say to you if you
were able to speak to Him face to face about your reservations right now?
(*For further study, read 1 Corinthians 1:18-31.*)

*Father, even though I often feel like the least of all of Your children,
I know that You have chosen me and love me in spite of how I see myself.
Thank You, Father, for sanctifying me daily while having justified me
already through Your Son's precious blood. Amen.*

Into Which Angels Long to Look

Ephesians 3:10

"So that through the church the manifold wisdom of God might now be made known to the rulers and authorities in the heavenly places."

When Peter spoke of this "manifold wisdom of God" that has been revealed to us, he said they were things "into which angels long to look." (1 Peter 1:12) Often we take for granted the beautiful truths that have been given to us by our Father. We live each of our days while here on this earth with a sort of nonchalant attitude in terms of the knowledge of Christ and salvation, forgetting that the very thought of this kind of wisdom and love is something that the heavenly beings themselves long to see.

What an awesome privilege we have been given in that God has chosen to display His glory and truth through us, His church. Paul is telling us here that we are the instruments by which God has demonstrated His wisdom to all these heavenly beings, both good and bad. We are the chosen vessels through whom He displays His truth. How can we but joyfully live in light of this tremendous heritage?

– Study/Meditation –

How should this knowledge affect the way we live
while on this earth? How should it affect the way we think
about our own salvation?

*Father, though I am unworthy, I thank You for choosing
one such as me to display Your glory and grace. Help me, Father,
to live a life that is worthy of such an honor. Amen.*

30

My Eternal Purpose

Ephesians 3:11-12

"This was according to the eternal purpose that he has realized in Christ Jesus our Lord, in whom we have boldness and access with confidence through our faith in him."

The concept of time is something we take for granted as human beings. Even our fairy tales begin with "Once upon a time…" It's so much ingrained in every facet of our lives that we generally don't give it a thought; we measure everything in terms of time. Yet, time doesn't exist with God, at least not in the way that we think of it, and so eternity for Him is the norm.

That's probably one of the reasons why it is so hard for us to fathom God's purposes for us having been established from an eternal perspective rather than a time-centered temporal one, but that is exactly what happened. God's purposes for His children were founded not at our birth or even at the birth of mankind; they were founded in eternity, and they were always founded in Christ. What a comforting knowledge to be assured that my eternity and my salvation existed long before me. How wonderful to know that God's plan for the place and existence of His church has simply always been. Let us take great joy in knowing our positions have always been secure.

– Study/Meditation –

Why do you think God created time for us? What does it mean that He exists outside of time?
(*For further study, read Psalm 139.*)

Father, You are eternal and glorious. You are too high for me to fathom, but I thank You for Your love and faithfulness to me. Thank You for choosing me before the foundation of time. Amen.

31

Bold Confidence

Ephesians 3:11-13

"This was according to the eternal purpose that he has realized in Christ Jesus our Lord, in whom we have boldness and access with confidence through our faith in him. So I ask you not to lose heart over what I am suffering for you, which is your glory."

How often do we, as believers, really think about the awesome privilege we have to boldly approach the Throne of Grace? In Christ, we have been given this privilege, the privilege of asking our Father for whatever is in our hearts, being confident that He is both listening and will answer according to His will. The beautiful thing about this fact is that His will is to work out all of these things for our good and His glory. Jesus said in John 15 that whatever we ask of the Father in His name, or anything in line with His character and will, those things will be given to us. Of course, that doesn't mean we get whatever we want as long as we ask it "in Jesus' name." What Jesus is saying and what Paul is referring to is the gift we have been given as God's children through Jesus Christ to be able to approach the Lord God, Creator of the Universe, and know that He is willing and able to answer us with love and mercy, and that His answer will always be good and right.

Additionally, it's often said that we see the true character of a person in the midst of crisis. When everything else is stripped away – all of the comforts and amenities of this life – what do we focus on as most important? Jesus promised us that we would suffer in this life, but we often act as though it's so terribly unexpected and unfair when exactly that happens to us. And more importantly, we often forget that God loves us and has also promised that He will work all things together for good for His people and according to His glory. (Romans 8:28) "All things" in any other language still means "all things." God is in the business of working in our lives, always, and that amazing truth must be what we see in the midst of any crisis. Paul demonstrated for the Ephesians, and for us, what it looks like to focus on the right things while we suffer, and those things are all about God.

– Study/Meditation –

Think of a time of crisis in your life. On what did you immediately focus? How can we grow so that our immediate focus is the glory of God?

Father, thank You for the assurances You give in Your Word that You are in control and working in my life. Help me to remember that random things do not happen to me, but that my life is in the hands of my loving and faithful Abba Father. Amen.

32

Childlike Prayer

Ephesians 3:14-15

"For this reason I bow my knees before the Father, from whom every family in heaven and on earth is named."

When you come to your Father in prayer, do you come as a pauper bowing before the rich ruler in hopes that He will bestow on you some blessing? Or do you come to the Lord as one who is part of His family and who knows what He has given you already? Paul reminds us in these few words how it is we are to approach the Throne of Grace in prayer.

When he said, "For this reason I bow my knees," to what reason is he referring? He is referring to what he has been saying in the two previous chapters – the enormity of God's plan of redemption and the reality of God's plan for His church. Paul is saying that he comes to God with his petitions remembering all that God has already done and all that God has promised to do for us, His family.

We come before our Father with our requests and petitions as a child who is dearly loved and cared for, and we come remembering what He has already accomplished on our behalf. We are not paupers before a harsh ruler; we are children before our Father.

– Study/Meditation –

What difference does it make when we come to God
as His children as opposed to as His subjects? How do you
approach Him in prayer?

*Father, I come to You today with my cares and concerns knowing
that You are my Father and my Lord. Thank You for bringing me into
Your family and for loving me as Your own. Amen.*

According to the Riches of His Glory

Ephesians 3:16

"That according to the riches of his glory he may grant you to be strengthened with power through his Spirit in your inner being."

Often we pray as if God's answers to our prayers are somehow inhibited by His ability to answer them. If it seems that He is saying "No" or even that He is silent, we might surmise that we haven't prayed hard enough or in the right words. Perhaps He misunderstood and we weren't clear enough. Perhaps what we're asking for is simply not possible.

The truth is, as Paul reminds us, that God is more than able and willing to answer our prayers. As a matter of fact, our prayers are always answered out of the manifold greatness of who He is. Our attitude of prayer should never be one that is asking God if He is able to do something; instead it should be coming to our Father and asking Him to align our wills with His so that we can see with more wisdom what is good and right in the answer.

Additionally, our attitudes should never be that we can pray a certain way – with more faith or eloquence – and God will give us what we desire. Remember that when Jesus, a Man who had never sinned or prayed incorrectly, prayed in the Garden of Gethsemane that the cup pass from Him, God's answer was "No." From that answer, millions of men and women from every tribe, nation, and tongue have come to know the one true living God. God is God and we must always approach Him with His character, not ours, in the center of our prayers.

(continued)

According to the Riches of His Glory – *continued*

– Study/Meditation –

Look closer at Jesus prayer in Matthew 6:9-13.
What can we learn from the way our Savior prayed?

**Father, I come to You in full knowledge of Your greatness,
asking You for (insert your requests here). Thank You for hearing me
and answering me. Father, give me the wisdom to see Your will in the
answer and to trust Your love as it comes to pass. Amen.*

34

Spiritual Muscles

Ephesians 3:16-17a

"That according to the riches of his glory he may grant you to be strengthened with power through his Spirit in your inner being, so that Christ may dwell in your hearts through faith."

As human beings, we work hard on our physical bodies. We diet, we exercise, we get check-ups from the doctor, and all to the end of taking care of our bodies. While this is necessary and good, we very often do so to the neglect of our inner beings, and it is toward this that Paul specifically prays for the Ephesians in this passage.

He is praying that they be strengthened in their inner beings by the Holy Spirit so that Christ might dwell there through faith. He prays that according to God's blessings and riches we might look to the indwelling Holy Spirit to give us spiritual muscles. Then these spiritual muscles will work out within our souls in order to build a proper and strong house for our Savior to dwell within our hearts. That simply means that the solid rock of our faith is built to that strength so that we are firm in our faith in Christ.

As the storms of life hit a man whose inner being is strengthened by the Holy Spirit according to God's riches so that Christ dwells within him, the wind and rain will beat unsuccessfully against a ballasted heart. Let us remember to pray for our inner being even as we pray for our outer selves; the former will live in eternity and is worthy of much attention now.

– Study/Meditation –

How do we "work out" our inner beings? What can you do each day in a practical sense to build up your spiritual self?

*Father, I pray today that You give me the wisdom to work on my heart and to make my soul a secure dwelling place for Your Son. Thank You for the Spirit who works in me toward this end. Amen.

Someone Who Looks Like Christ

Ephesians 3:17b -19

"That you, being rooted and grounded in love, may have the strength to comprehend with all the saints what is the breadth and length and height and depth, and to know the love of Christ that surpasses knowledge, that you may be filled with all the fullness of God."

When someone looks at you, do they immediately think, "Now, there's someone who looks like Christ"? That is a tall order for fallen creatures such as ourselves, but we are called to become more and more like our Savior as we are sanctified daily toward the glorification of our mortal bodies. The only possible way we can ever be more like Christ is if our hearts are made into a proper dwelling place for Jesus, which is why Paul is praying this particular prayer for the Ephesians, and for us. The beautiful result of this prayer being answered, that we have a heart where our Savior dwells, is that we, along with all of the saints, can better understand how magnificent is our Savior and how unsearchable is His love for us.

Paul prays that we might understand what is "the breadth and length and height and depth" of this love. These terms of measurement are reminiscent of the language he used in 2:21 about each believer being part of the whole of the temple of God in Christ, wherein as part of this temple we also understand the fullness of the God who created it. He is praying that we have spiritual maturity, because only there will we truly know Who it is that we serve and how much we are loved by so great a King. It is on this road to spiritual maturity that others can look at us and say, "Now, there's someone who looks like Christ."

– Study/Meditation –

If the spiritual temple of God is made up of individual members
of the body of Christ, then why is it important that we understand that Jesus
is the cornerstone of this temple? How does knowing this help facilitate our
understanding the fullness of God?

*Father, help me today to better understand Your character
and Your love so that I may continue on my quest for spiritual maturity.
Thank You for loving me so completely. Amen.*

My Healthy Prayer Life

Ephesians 3:20-21

"Now to him who is able to do far more abundantly than all that we ask or think, according to the power at work within us, to him be glory in the church and in Christ Jesus throughout all generations, forever and ever."

When you sit in prayer, do you ever worry that you might leave something out or forget to pray something? Often many of us keep prayer journals, which should serve to keep us focused throughout our time with God. However, sometimes we see them more as a means of keeping us from forgetting something, as if forgetting to mention something to God means He won't give us what we need or take care of us.

We must remember that our Father, this great and awesome God that we serve, is greater than all that we know, and as Paul reminds us, He can do far more than we could ever ask or think. He knows what we need before we do, and our limited humanity will never impede nor dissuade His sovereign hand. God will be glorified and He will accomplish His purposes through us and through His church. Let us take comfort in having a Father who knows us so completely and works far outside of our humanity and the limitations therein.

– Study/Meditation –

What is the purpose of prayer if God knows what we need
long before we do? If Jesus is God, then why do you think He prayed?
(For further study, look at the Lord's Prayer in Matthew 6:9-13.
What does Jesus tell us in this prayer that might answer the above questions?)

Father, I lay my requests and petitions at Your feet, thanking You for knowing me and what I need even if I don't. You are glorious in Your sovereign majesty and I praise You in all of the answers, even the ones I ask incorrectly or leave out entirely. Thank You, God. Amen.

37

Walk the Talk!

Ephesians 4:1

"I therefore, a prisoner for the Lord, urge you to walk in a manner worthy of the calling to which you have been called."

Paul has been exhorting the Ephesian church about its membership in the family of God and that God is in control of all that happens to them, good or bad. Now he is going to spend the rest of his letter exhorting them on how to live as those who have been given such an amazing gift.

Not surprisingly, the first thing he writes in respect to this exhortation is that their lives effectively mirror the great call they have received. He tells them to "walk in a manner worthy" of this gift of being grafted into the family of God. In essence, Paul is saying, "Walk your talk!" The position in Christ that we have been freely given is of great worth; it is eternal. How are we to live out the Great Commission given us by our Savior if our lives don't demonstrate to the world how great a gift is salvation? The world is watching us! There is often no greater witness than our lives, and Paul is rightly reminding us that we must live a life that reflects the great worth of what we have been given. Walk the talk, and live the gift.

– Study/Meditation –

How can you, on a day to day basis, more effectively "walk the talk"?
Why is it so important that you do so?

Father, I praise You for the magnificent gift of being part of Your family and receiving eternal life. Give me the wisdom and patience and love to manifest You to a world that is dying without You. Amen.

Bearing with My Brothers and Sisters

Ephesians 4:2

"(Walk) with all humility and gentleness, with patience, bearing with one another in love."

We have such high expectations of our fellow brothers and sisters, don't we? It's there that we expect to be treated fairly and with dignity and respect, and when one of them fails in that, we can be very deeply offended with them. Paul, however, tells us that living in a manner worthy of the call placed on our lives is defined by the way we treat others, not by the way they treat us.

Humility and gentleness must exist in the face of the King of kings, but by His example, it must also exist as we deal with one another. Jesus washed His disciples' feet; we can't expect to treat fellow Christians with any less humility and gentleness. Being patient with each other while both enduring and forgiving any wrongs are equally necessary, and all of this is about how we treat them, not about how they treat us. That is love, and that is by what Jesus said the world would know us.

The life we must live that is worthy of being in the family of God is to love the family of God, being humble and gentle, patient and loving. Remember, your call is based on what you do, not on what others do to you.

– Study/Meditation –

How do you think you can improve in this call on your life?
What does it mean to treat fellow brothers and sisters as family?
(For further study, read Genesis 37. How does this family show us the opposite of what Paul is explaining?)

Father, please forgive me for the times I have mistreated my Christian family. Help me to keep myself out of the picture and to instead consider others more important. Amen.

Unity

Ephesians 4:3

"(Walk) eager to maintain the unity of the Spirit in the bond of peace."

There is something fundamentally satisfying to the human psyche when we are correct in an argument. We feel justified in our opinions or actions at that moment, and we feel generally good about ourselves. Unfortunately, sometimes we seek that feeling to the detriment of unity in the body of believers. Sometimes our goal is not unity, as Paul calls us to in maintaining and walk worthy of the call of Christ, but instead our goal can be to be right in a dispute or argument. No one, including Paul, is suggesting that we are going to agree on everything just because we share belief in Christ. We are family, after all, and one generally argues with his/her family more than anyone else.

The point Paul is making is that our goal should be unity above anything else. Once again, a dying world is watching us. If the only thing they see is backstabbing and arguing amongst a people who supposedly share the most blessed and gracious gift known to mankind, why would they want to be a part of that family? Part of living the life we are called to live as believers is having a goal of unity and love with each other. It's not always possible, but as Paul also said, inasmuch as it is possible for you, live in peace with your brothers and sisters.

– Study/Meditation –

Think of a disagreement either you are involved in now or have been in the past with a fellow believer? If an unbeliever were observing this disagreement, would God have been glorified in the way it played out? How might you change any part of it if you had it to do over again?

*Father, please forgive me of my pride when I seek to "win" an argument. Help me to love unconditionally and to seek peace with my family. When I do disagree, help me to do so lovingly and without malice, bringing You glory and honor in all things. Amen.

One Body

Ephesians 4:4-6

"There is one body and one Spirit – just as you were called to one hope that belongs to your call – one Lord, one faith, one baptism, one God and Father of all, who is over all and through all and in all."

As Paul continues to exhort us on unity among believers, it is interesting here that he does not use the analogy of a "family" to express this sentiment, but a "body." Why do you think that is so? A family is a unified structure who are all related, so why a body?

The reason is that Paul is trying to convey the very essence and need of unity among believers, and that is truly expressed best in terms of a body. Every part is necessary for the whole and every part must work in conjunction with the whole so that the body functions properly. In a family, that is not always nor necessarily the case. The Church of our Lord, Jesus Christ, is a body that is brought together by one Spirit, one Lord, one faith, and one baptism. No matter what church you go to, if it professes and practices a true faith in Jesus Christ as their Savior, those people are also part of the body. We may not share in particular facets of belief, but we are still joined by one core – Jesus.

We must seek not only to operate as a body within our local church but also within the church. It should never be building against building or denomination against denomination. Good discussion about differences in nuances of doctrine is good. However, dissention and backstabbing because of differences in nuances of doctrine are sowing discord among brothers, and the Word states that our Lord hates that. (Proverbs 6:19) Let us seek unity with one another, bound by one Lord.

– Study/Meditation –

How is disunity in the body often played out these days
in terms of differences of doctrine? How can these differences exist
in a healthy, but unified, way?

Father, help me not to foster disunity amongst my brethren.
Give me the patience and wisdom I need to treat everyone in the
Body of Christ as members of my family and to do all that
I can to live in harmony with them. Amen.

Gifts in the Body

Ephesians 4:7
*"But grace was given to each one of us according
to the measure of Christ's gifts."*

Paul has been speaking specifically about unity in the body of believers up to this point, but now he seems to take a turn to begin speaking of the diversities that also exist there. He is now going to spend the next set of verses speaking of the differing gifts given to each believer. However, notice that even a discussion of these different gifts begins with a unified state – all of us have been given grace through our Lord Jesus Christ and in that we have been given gifts.

Additionally, though we have all been given individual gifts, these gifts are given so that the whole may be served. It's still really about unity. God's manifold grace has been bestowed on all of His children so that eternity is theirs, and one of the ways in which this grace has been granted is through the delegation of the gifts. These gifts are then to be used to build up the body. Once again, the analogy of a "body" becomes clear in that we have received everything from our Father so the living organism that is the church functions effectively for the advancement of the Kingdom of God.

– Study/Meditation –

How are God's grace and the bestowment of His gifts compared?
How is properly using our spiritual gifts dependent on God's grace?

*Father, help me to identify what gift You have given me and then show
me where best to use it for Your glory and the advancement of Your Kingdom.
Thank You for the grace so that I may be used by You. Amen.*

A Great Humility

Ephesians 4:8-10

"Therefore it says, 'When he ascended on high he led a host of captives, and he gave gifts to men.' (In saying, 'He ascended,' what does it mean but that he had also descended into the lower parts of the earth? He who descended is the one who also ascended far above all the heavens, that he might fill all things.)"

These few verses can be very confusing, and in that confusion, it can also be difficult to make application to our lives. However, a short explanation will make application much easier. The reference Paul is making in verse 8 is from Psalm 68 where the psalmist is proclaiming God's triumphal march from Mount Sinai in the wilderness to Mount Zion in Jerusalem. Paul is making a comparison between this occasion and the ascent of Jesus into heaven.

He goes on to explain in verses 9-10 that Christ's "descent" was His incarnation into humanity on earth with the culmination occurring in His ascension to heaven. Why would he pause to tell his readers this in the middle of a discussion of gifts and unity? Simply put, Paul wants to frame this discussion with the source of our spiritual gifts – Christ – and more specifically, with Christ's humility and sacrifice in supplying these gifts. Everything we are given is in light of Christ and the Kingdom of God. There is no room for pride or self-serving actions. The beginning and the end is our Lord. Everything about us, including our giftings, are His and must always be used to His service.

(continued)

42

A Great Humility – *continued*

– Study/Meditation –

How can meditating on Christ's particular sacrifice of laying aside
His throne in heaven so that He might live as a man on this earth help
you to better serve Him with your gifts?

*Father, thank You for sending Your Son to this earth to live as a man
so that I might live in eternity. Help me to keep that humility in the
forefront of my mind as I live to serve You here. Amen.*

43

Called to the Work of the Church

Ephesians 4:11-12

"And he gave the apostles, the prophets, the evangelists,
the pastors and teachers to equip the saints for the work of ministry,
for building up the body of Christ."

There's an old saying: "10% of the people do 100% of the work." That is unfortunately often true in the church, as well. What is even more unfortunate is that many times that 10% are staff members, or even worse, the pastors and teachers of the church doing most of the work. It is a common misconception that God's calling on the lives of some to be pastors, teachers, evangelists and the like is a call to "work" in the church. The belief is that God has given them a special gifting that enables them to complete His work in the most beneficial fashion. Yet, Paul doesn't say that these people are called to "work" in the church; he says they are called to "equip the saints for the work of ministry."

Your pastors and teachers and leaders of your local church are not called to do the work of ministry; they are called to equip *you* to do the work of ministry. Once again, that is why Paul uses the analogy of a body; each of us has a part to play in this work of ministry. You are a member of the saints who are called to God's work. Take direction and training from your pastors and teachers, but then take the work they train you to do. In this way, we are all working parts of the Body of Christ.

(continued)

43

Called to the Work of the Church – continued

– Study/Meditation –

Paul lists many other gifts of the Spirit in Romans 12:3-8
and 1 Corinthians 12:1-11. Though these lists are in no way exhaustive,
how are the leaders of the church "equipping" the saints with these gifts
for works of service? Which are your gifts and how are you using them?

Father, thank You for calling many to lead us in Your church.
Thank You for the call on their lives to equip us to do Your work.
Help me to learn from them and then to step out and do my part in the Body.
Forgive me for the times I haven't done my part and give me
the wisdom and courage I need to do it. Amen.

The Unity of Faith

Ephesians 4:13

"...until we all attain to the unity of the faith and of the knowledge of the Son of God, to mature manhood, to the measure of the stature of the fullness of Christ."

Paul is now completing his thoughts on the purpose for elders and pastors and teachers. He said in the previous two verses that they are given to the church to build them up and to equip them for service to God's Kingdom. Now he explains why – why is it necessary that the body of Christ be equipped to this end?

Once again the goal is unity which results in spiritual maturity and in full knowledge of our Savior. Paul said we must be equipped "until we all attain to the unity of the faith." It is so very unfortunate that some of the greatest disputes among believers today is with each other. Paul is telling us that we are being equipped to serve in the Kingdom so that we can attain the unity we must have with each other that is founded in our faith in Jesus Christ. It is the tie that binds us and secures us together with our Lord in eternity. This unity of faith is tied to a knowledge of Jesus, which we also attain as we serve together, leading to spiritual maturity and a full realization of Him.

We serve in the Kingdom, as we are equipped to do, so that we can be unified one to another, in faith and knowledge of Him we serve. Only then do we become more like Him and know more of Him.

(continued)

The Unity of Faith

Why is "unity of faith" so important among believers? What is the very sad result when believers do not seek to attain this unity? Why do you think service is key to attaining unity of faith?

Father, thank You for continually sanctifying me in Your Word. Help me to boldly serve others in Your Kingdom to Your service, and give me the wisdom to seek unity with my brothers and sisters. Amen.

Do I Know What I Know?

Ephesians 4:14

*"So that we may no longer be children, tossed to and fro
by the waves and carried about by every word of doctrine, by
human cunning, by craftiness in deceitful schemes."*

Every parent worries about their children being tricked and taken advantage of by an ill-willed adult. We worry that in their immaturity, their discernment is lacking and they are, therefore, easy targets. In a spiritual sense, adults are just as vulnerable to deceitful ideas if they remain immature in their beliefs and their knowledge of the truth.

Paul is reminding us that God gifted pastors and teachers and the like in the church to equip us not only to serve in the Kingdom, but to build us up in the knowledge of the truth of the Gospel so that we are discerning. Only then can we be armed against false doctrines and lies about God and His Word. There are so many nuances out there that to the human ear sound fine; they may even make a measure of sense. If we don't know in our hearts the Word of God and the truth therein, we won't have a baseline in which to discern when these things are lies or when they are not. Only the Bible is inerrant. Only God's Word stands tried and true. We must be built up there so that our wisdom supersedes the lies of the enemy.

– Study/Meditation –

What can you do personally, on a day to day basis, which can
help you be discerning in terms of spiritual truths? Why is this so important?
(*For further study, read Colossians 2:6-15.*)

*Father, thank You for giving us Your Word to guide us. Forgive me
for not spending as much time there as I should and help me see Your
truths in it so that I might become more discerning. Amen.*

46

Truth and Love

Ephesians 4:15

*"Rather, speaking the truth in love, we are to grow up in
every way into him who is the head, into Christ."*

Rather than what? Paul is telling us what we should be doing in our quest for unity and spiritual maturity – becoming more and more like Christ – rather than being swayed by false doctrine and the schemes of man. But he gives another qualification here, and it is of the utmost importance. We are to "speak the truth in love." These two things are not mutually exclusive actions. They exist together; in fact, they must exist together so that we can grow up in every way to be like our Savior.

Yes, we must love truth and we must seek truth. We mustn't be tossed to and fro by every wind of doctrine or scheme of man, and we must guard each other against such things. And yes, the way to combat lies is truth. However, truth without love is like anything without love; Paul calls these things in 1 Corinthians 13:1 a clanging symbol. Being a lover of truth without love is of no service to the Kingdom. Likewise, love without truth is useless; as a matter of fact, an argument can be made that it's not love at all. Real love seeks that which is good for the recipient, and truth is good. Real love will do and say the hard things because of love and in love. Therefore, our growth as individuals in Christ and as the body of Christ will be based in both of these things – truth and love.

– Study/Meditation –

What does it mean on a day to day basis to speak the truth
in love to each other? What is an example of truth without love and
love without truth? How would both of these instances be detrimental
to growing in the Kingdom of God?

*Father, help me to speak the truth in love. Help me to understand what that
means as I live and grow with my fellow believers. And help me receive truth in
love, discerning that it is good for me and for the body of Christ. Amen.*

47

Being Part of the Whole

Ephesians 4:16

"(Christ), from whom the whole body, joined and held together by every joint with which it is equipped, when each part is working properly, makes the body grow so that it builds itself up in love."

Each of us is a part of the whole. We are all part of the Body of Christ, but we often have a hard time truly seeing ourselves as a "part." Instead, it's a lot more natural for us to view ourselves in terms of being a whole unto ourselves. We respond according to self, we act according to self, we make decisions according to self. It is completely outside of human nature to do otherwise.

However, Paul has been reminding us that we are really parts that must work together so that the whole can grow. The purpose of the Church is to grow together so that God may be glorified in the world. It is not about how wonderfully spiritual you are or that I am; it's about how our spiritual growth affects and contributes to the growth of the Body. That's why it is all about service to one another and love for one another and unity with one another. The end result of individual parts growing for this purpose is a mature and affective Body of Christ.

– Study/Meditation –

How should your spiritual growth manifest itself in the Body of Christ?
What is the end result if every member of the Body did the same?

Father, help me to see my part in the function of the Body and to boldly step forward and do it. Help me to be selfless and to seek that which is right for the Kingdom, even if it is not necessarily comfortable for me. Amen.

Do Not Walk as Those Who Do Not Know

Ephesians 4:17-19

"Now this I say and testify in the Lord, that you must no longer walk as the Gentiles do, in the futility of their minds. They are darkened in their understanding, alienated from the life of God because of the ignorance that is in them, due to their hardness of heart. They have become callous and have given themselves up to sensuality, greedy to practice every kind of impurity."

Whereas Paul's directive for us to "no longer walk as the Gentiles do" seems self-descriptive, there is a phrase in these verses that explains where humanity goes wrong every time. The "Gentiles" were people who did not believe in Christ, and we are called to walk differently than they do, but what is it about being a Gentile that results in wrong living? Paul uses the phrase, "in the futility of their minds." That is, the thing that separates a child of God from everyone else is who lives in us – the Holy Spirit. Without Him, the only other guide we have is ourselves, our minds, and since they are depraved by nature, it is futile to think we would do anything other than depraved things.

Paul is saying that we must no longer live a life as one who has only himself to hear. We have God, the Holy Spirit, guiding us, and therefore ignorance and hardness of heart and callous behavior are defeated. Our understanding is no longer darkened, so we must not live as if it is. Life is not futile in Jesus Christ. Why live like it is?

How is our thinking futile if not guided by the Holy Spirit?
Why is an unbeliever "darkened "in his understanding?
(*For further study, read 1 Corinthians 1:18-25.*)

*Father, thank You for coming into my heart and giving
me the light of the truth. I know that without You I would be
utterly lost and my life would be futile. To You I give all the
glory and honor and praise. I love You! Thank You for
loving me first. Amen.*

49

The Replacements Given By Christ

Ephesians 4:20-21

"But that is not the way you learned Christ! – assuming that you have heard about him and were taught in him, as the truth is in Jesus."

Remember the key phrase from yesterday's verses that describe how the unbeliever lives? Paul called it living "in the futility of their minds." They are their own guides to living, hearing and following the pointless direction of their own thinking. We would do the same, were it not for what Paul points out in these next two verses – Christ.

And notice that it is all about Christ: learning Him, hearing of Him, taught in Him, and truth that is in Him. Whereas without Jesus we are about ourselves and thereby destined to live in futility, with Christ we live because of and for Someone greater. Once we have a Savior, we also have a Guide. This Guide shines the light of truth on our understanding, taking away our heart of stone and replacing it with a heart of flesh. We are then no longer hard and callous, but now have within us a love that far in a way surpasses evil.

There is nothing futile about the life of a Christian because that life is about Jesus. Hope replaces futility, love replaces hate, and eternity replaces death.

– Study/Meditation –

What does it mean for a believer to "learn Christ"? How might we do this?

Father, thank You for changing my heart of stone into a heart of flesh.
Thank You for loving me so much that You were willing to show me
the light of Truth. Thank You for the hope that lives in Jesus
and thereby lives in me. Amen.

Walking the Walk

Ephesians 4:22

". . . to put off your old self, which belongs to your former manner of life and is corrupt through deceitful desires. . ."

There is an old saying: "Walk the walk; don't just talk the talk." In essence, that is what Paul is reminding us of in this verse. He had previously pointed out that the person without Christ will live according to his own depraved nature, "darkened in their understanding" and with "hardness of heart." He said that believers, however, didn't learn Christ that way. Instead there is a moral component to being a Christian. Once we have accepted Jesus Christ as our Savior and the Holy Spirit comes to dwell in our hearts, our lives will change, and this change will be reflected in our behavior.

No, we are not saved because of our moral behavior, but our moral behavior will change because we are saved. No longer are we led by our deceitful desires, but now we have within us the Comforter, the Advisor, the One who gives us the ability, as well as the desire, to truly walk the walk.

– Study/Meditation –

How does what Paul is teaching in this verse mirror what
Jesus taught in John 3 about being born again?
(For further study, read John 3:1-8.)

*Father, help me today as I endeavor to live according to
Your laws and ways. Help me listen to the Spirit and not my nature,
truly putting off my old self and exhibiting for others what the new
person in Christ looks like. Amen.*

The Renewed Mind

Ephesians 4:23-24

"That you be renewed in the spirit of your mind, and put on the new self, which in the likeness of God has been created in righteousness and holiness of truth."

Sin and corrupt behavior most certainly begin in the mind, and if we want to see significant change, the mind is exactly where it must begin. God, in His sovereign and holy omniscience, does begin there by renewing our minds first. The truest blessing for the believer is that she is no longer held captive by a depraved and sinful mind; she has been renewed! John called it being "regenerated" and Paul called it being "resurrected," but both mean we are made new from the inside out!

This new mind, or new self, is in the likeness of God Himself and is founded on the very essence of His righteousness and His holiness. It is an imputed righteousness, but it is imputed to us. In that, then, we seek to follow and remember to Whom we belong and by Whom we were created and in Whose likeness we were renewed. Hallelujah and Amen!

– Study/Meditation –

What does it mean to have an "imputed" righteousness?
How should this better dictate our lives while on this earth?
(For further study, read Romans 6.)

Father, thank You for making me new. I love You! Amen.

52

Putting on the New Self

Ephesians 4:25

"Therefore, having put away falsehood, let each one of you speak the truth with his neighbor, for we are members of one another."

One of the very first things that accompanies the "new self" we put on in Christ is a desire for truth, and yet lying has become such a pervading aspect of our culture that we often do it without even thinking. Even our entertainment is fraught with half-truths and deceptions – buy this perfume and you'll find the man of your dreams, own this car and your life will be complete, wear these jeans and your day will be bright. It sounds ludicrous, but it is such a part of mainstream culture that we live in it without thinking of it.

However, Paul's admonition to take off the old nature and put on the new one is followed almost immediately with a reminder that truth and truth-telling must become as natural to us as any other part of our new existences. Why? For the same reason that Paul has been entreating us toward in all of Ephesians: for the sake of unity in Christ. He says we must speak the truth "for we are members of one another." Truth builds up and lies tear down. Let us continually seek to put off the old self and to put on the new, treating one another with love and respect, and let us begin by putting away falsehood and speaking the truth in love.

– Study/Meditation –

What does "speak the truth in love" mean in a believer's relationship with other believers? How can this mandate be misused? What must we do to insure that we are following Paul's directions here correctly?

Father, help me in my constant struggle to put off my old nature. Help me to surrender my thoughts and words to You, because only there can I find victory. Thank You for continuing to sanctify me daily. Amen.

53

Is it Okay to be Angry?

Ephesians 4:26-27

*"Be angry and do not sin; do not let the sun go down on your anger,
and give no opportunity to the devil."*

"Be angry and do not sin." Those are some of the most humanly revealing words ever given by Paul. We are a people of emotion. We were created by and in the image of a God of emotion. We're going to feel anger and pain and hurt and love and passion. It's what we do with those emotions, however, that will determine whether or not they become sinful.

Our anger is sometimes rightfully felt and sometimes unrightfully felt, but in either case we must seek to remain sinless in that anger. Paul, ever the practical advisor, even goes on to tell us how to facilitate that end. He tells us not to let the sun go down on our anger. In other words, he's saying, "You're going to get angry occasionally, but you mustn't sin in that anger. The way to keep from sinning in your anger is to not allow it to harbor in your heart. Don't let the day end without making peace, either with yourself or with others."

Once we allow anger to fester in our hearts, it turns quickly into bitterness and revengefulness; sin follows rapidly thereafter. Paul is continuing to tell us how to have unity among ourselves, and handling our anger in a righteous manner is paramount therein. As the writer of Hebrews tells us, "Strive for peace with everyone." (Hebrews 12:14)

According to Paul, anger in and of itself is not wrong.
How do we make it wrong? What are some things we can do so
that the sun does not go down on our anger? What do you personally
need to do so that you do not sin in your anger?

*Father, thank You for giving me emotions. Thank You for the ability
to feel as I am created in Your image. Help me not to sin in those emotions,
keeping You and Your Word ever forefront in my mind. Amen.*

What We Do Matters

Ephesians 4:28

"Let the thief no longer steal, but rather let him labor, doing honest work with his own hands, so that he may have something to share with anyone in need."

Paul is making two sweeping points here, and if we're not careful, we may step right past them in generalities rather than glean from the specific things he says. The apostle does speak to thieves in this verse, but he is using that sin as an example. If one is a thief, Paul says for that person to change his or her actions and work for their money. The key thing is changing one's actions.

Whatever sin has characterized our lives before we became part of the body of Christ must change to actions that instead mirror Christ. Sin cannot continue in the temple where the Holy Spirit dwells.

The second point Paul is making speaks again to unity in the body. Every action in which we engage must ultimately build up the body of Christ. Everything about us after conversion is about God, His glory, and the building up of His Church. We can only do that as we remove the old self and put on the new. As Paul illustrates here, that will be reflected in our outward actions.

– Study/Meditation –

Look closer at the last part of verse 28. In what way does Paul address our intentions in our actions? Why do you think that is important?

Father, thank You for sanctifying me daily. Help me to see the things in my life that must change so that I more clearly demonstrate Your glory to the world; then give me the strength to change those things so that my life is more pleasing to You. Amen.

55

My Words Matter

Ephesians 4:29

"Let no corrupting talk come out of your mouths, but only such as is good for building up, as fits the occasion, that it may give grace to those who hear."

So often we think of "corrupting talk" as foul language or irreverent speech. However, the very essence of the word "corrupt" means "spoiled" or "decayed." Our speech is corrupt any time is spoils that which the Father intends for His glory and our good. Our speech lacks integrity when its end is only the decaying of a situation or even of a person.

The world ought to hear the words from our mouths and think, "I want to be a Christian." The world should hear what we say to one another and think, "These people are bound together in love and unity by a good and loving God." Paul is reminding us that our words matter, and they matter all of the time. We must become more aware of our speech and of our words, only speaking those things which build each other up and promote unity amongst the brethren. Only in this way will we bring glory to our Heavenly Father and His Kingdom.

– Study/Meditation –

Why do you think James referred to the tongue as a "restless evil"?
Why did Jesus say that out of a man's mouth his heart is revealed?
What should our words say about our hearts?

Father, keep me ever mindful of the words that I speak. Help me to be sanctified in my speech, saying only those things that bring You glory and build up Your Kingdom. Amen.

Living as a Temple

Ephesians 4:30

"And do not grieve the Holy Spirit of God, by whom you were sealed for the day of redemption."

It is a serious directive not to grieve the Holy Spirit. Paul is distinctly pointing out the difference between God's presence in the lives of His children in the Old Testament and His presence in their lives in the New Testament.

In the Old Testament, God's presence was manifested in a cloud or in fire that would dwell in the temple. Now, since the resurrection of Christ, God has given us the Holy Spirit to dwell "in" us; we are the temple. Therefore, the Spirit lives within us, listening to and witnessing every thought and word and deed.

How our speech and actions must often offend Him! Paul is reminding us that we are responsible for our words and deeds in Christ. A good measuring rod for us is to be reminded that God the Holy Spirit is in us; He is with us every minute of every day witnessing all that we do and say. If we were to but keep this fact in the forefront of our minds, it would make us more conscious of saying and doing the right things.

– Study/Meditation –

Think of a situation where recently you may have grieved
the Holy Spirit in your speech. How might you have handled
that situation differently?

*Father, please help me to be mindful of the things I do and say.
Help me not to grieve the Holy Spirit in my life, but instead to be a
pleasing aroma to You. Amen.*

57

Living as One Forgiven

Ephesians 4:31-32

*"Let all bitterness and wrath and anger and clamor
and slander be put away from you, along with all malice.
Be kind to one another, tenderhearted, forgiving one
another, as God in Christ forgave you."*

It is no accident in these last two verses of chapter 4 that Paul only uses personal action words: bitterness, wrath, anger, clamor, slander, malice, kind, tenderhearted, forgiving. All of these words require us to act in a certain way, and interestingly, other than the one used in terms of our direct response to God, not one of them is a contingency action. In other words, Paul doesn't say, "Put away bitterness and wrath if the offending party apologizes." He doesn't tell us, "Be kind to one another as long as they are kind to you." On the contrary, these are all actions that we are required to do, regardless of what others do to us.

God will only discuss you with you on Judgment Day. He will not ask you about your neighbor except in regards to how you treated him. Paul tells us how a person with a perfect eternity ought to respond to the temporary imperfections of this world – we do so with love and patience and kindness and forgiveness, and we do so because this has all been given to us and more.

– Study/Meditation –

Why is it so difficult for us to follow these simple instructions at times?
(*Hint: Who has become most important to me when I can't do what Paul says in these verses?*) What can we do to combat these tendencies?

*Father, You are glorious and magnificent and gracious and forgiving.
Help me to remember that all things are about You and Your Kingdom and not
my temporary woes. Help me to remember that You have given me eternity with
You so that all other things pale in comparison. Thank You, my Father. Amen.*

58

An Imitator of God

Ephesians 5:1-2

*"Therefore be imitators of God, as beloved children.
And walk in love, as Christ loved us and gave himself up for us,
a fragrant offering and sacrifice to God."*

It's often been said that "love" is an action word, and that is true. What we sometimes forget is that "love" is an action word whose action is pointed outward, not inward. We show love by giving love away, not by doing things in order to receive love. Therefore, at its very essence, love is completely and totally selfless, seeking the good of others. It is sacrificial, often meaning that in giving it we must give up something for ourselves.

Paul begins chapter 5, after explaining to us the differences between our old natures and the new ones we put on in Christ, by saying we should be imitators of God. That's a high calling, but it's a call to be holy, to be set apart, to not be like the world out of which we came. The only way we can do that is to walk in the love of Christ, which is real love, a love that exists outside of self for others. This is a call to be selfless. This is a call to put aside our natures which would otherwise seek only self-gratification and to instead seek that which is good for the Body of Christ, the Kingdom of God. Yes, it is a high call, but it is possible in the One who calls us to it. Therefore we must pray as Augustine did: "Lord, ask what You will, but grant what You ask."

– Study/Meditation –

When Jesus said that we must be holy as our Father in Heaven is holy,
what did He mean? How can we, as imperfect sinners, accomplish such a thing?

*Father, help me today to give love sacrificially to my fellow brothers
and sisters, thinking not of myself but of others. Give me the grace
to do what You command me to do. Amen.*

59

Remembering Who We Are

Ephesians 5:3-4

"But sexual immorality and all impurity or covetousness must not even be named among you, as is proper among saints. Let there be no filthiness nor foolish talk nor crude joking, which are out of place, but instead let there be thanksgiving."

It's a funny thing how differently we behave and even speak when we enter the church building. Very seldom would we tell a coarse joke or do something impure while there, but often it is a little easier to do so when outside of the building. Why is that? Simply put, we often forget that the "church building" is little more than just that – a building. What we need to remember is that our bodies are the temple of God. We, ourselves, house the Holy Spirit and to that end we must treat our physical bodies and minds as such.

With that in mind, engaging in any kind of immorality, particularly of a sexual nature, takes on an entirely more disturbing reality. Paul is reminding us in this next section that all forms of impurity in the life of a believer are a defiling of God's temple and shouldn't even be named among us. If we would but remember that there is no such thing as a moment when God isn't with us, we might be more cognizant of the temple in which we live and treat it as such.

– Study/Meditation –

Solomon once said that there is nothing new under the sun.
How is this truth conveyed in Paul's directives in these verses? How
is remembering that we are the very temple of God helpful in also
remembering what is and is not proper behavior for us?

*Father, forgive me for the times I have treated this temple
improperly and help me to treat it as holy. Thank You for Your
grace and forgiveness. Amen.*

The Issue with Sexual Sin

Ephesians 5:5-7

"For you may be sure of this, that everyone who is sexually immoral or impure, or who is covetous (that is, an idolater), has no inheritance in the kingdom of Christ and God. Let no one deceive you with empty words, for because of these things the wrath of God comes upon the sons of disobedience. Therefore do not associate with them."

It is true that sin, especially sexual sin, can sometimes look very attractive. We can reason it out, even convincing ourselves that it is okay, that no one will be hurt by this one act. And yet, God's Word is very explicit and exact on the destructive nature of this sin, even telling us that those who make it a practice of committing sexual sins are not going to receive the blessings of God's Kingdom.

These are serious warnings, and today's society doesn't think this way. As a matter of fact, these "sons of disobedience" to whom we are not to listen are represented by the world, a world that tells us daily that it's not that bad, that everyone's doing it, that it won't really hurt anyone. Sexual sin has become such a part of mainstay society that unless we maintain a strong tie to God's truths, we'll easily be swept away by its empty words. Paul says, "Therefore do not associate with them." Stay away from it and anyone who practices it. Instead, stay rooted in truth, in blessing, and in purity. The joy we seek can only be found there.

– Study/Meditation –

Why do you think Paul is addressing the Ephesians,
a people whom he already called recipients of the inheritance of God,
about what would make a person have no inheritance in God's Kingdom?
What does the fact that he warns them of this tell us today?

*Father, give me wisdom in this world to dwell only in
Your Word and in Your truths. Protect me from the lies
of the enemy and the lies of sin. Help me to remember
that the only true joy is found in You. Amen.*

I Am a Child of Light

Ephesians 5:8

"For at one time you were darkness, but now you are light in the Lord. Walk as children of light."

One of the most beautiful stories in the Bible is found in Luke 7 with the woman who washes Jesus' feet with her tears and dries them with her hair. She hears that Jesus will be at Simon's house, a Pharisee, so she goes there simply to worship Him. However, in the face of her sin, she becomes like Isaiah in Isaiah 6 and is overcome by who she is in light of who Jesus is, and she can do nothing but cry at His feet. Yet Simon, who was extremely self-righteous, was only indignant that Jesus even allowed this woman to sit at His feet, much less feel any remorse over his own state of sin.

Jesus used this situation to illustrate what Paul is saying to us in verse 8: it is vitally important that we remember who we were so that we properly appreciate who we now are. And notice that Paul remarks toward who we are, not where we are. He says that at one time we were darkness, not that we were in darkness, and that now we are light, not that we are in the light. God has changed us at our cores; He has made it possible to walk in this new identity, to walk as children of light.

Remember who you were so that you can live in who you are, and know that only God could have changed your heart so completely.

– Study/Meditation –

How does remembering who we were without Christ help us live as those who know Him now? (*Hint: Read Luke 7:36-50.*)

Father, thank You for changing my heart and making me a child of light. Help me to remember what You accomplished in my life so that I can live as Your child ought to live.
Amen.

The Fruit of Light

Ephesians 5:9-10

"For the fruit of light is found in all that is good and right and true. And try to discern what is pleasing to the Lord."

Paul had just said in the previous verse that we are now children of light and that we should walk in that light. Now he tells us that if we do, we will bear fruit that testifies to being children of light. Jesus said that good trees bear good fruit and that bad trees bear bad fruit. We will behave and say things that reflect what sort of tree we are, and since we have been changed into light, our fruit will be of the light. It will be good – without malice and generally seeking the welfare of others; it will be righteous – having the characteristic of things right before God; and it will be true – without falsehood and with integrity. Are we manifesting the light that we are in our daily lives by bearing this kind of fruit? As believers, we should be, and therefore we must seek to do so.

As Paul continues in verse ten, we realize that we don't have to try to discern what is pleasing to ourselves; that comes naturally enough. However, we cannot naturally discern what is pleasing to God. Because of that, Paul's basic instruction for us is simple a reminder that it takes effort to do so. And understand that he is not saying, "Just try and do it because you can't." What he is saying is, "Put all your effort into knowing those things that please your Father in heaven, and do so because He is your Father." In love and devotion to the Lord, it should be our deepest desire to please Him. Since that takes spiritual discernment and my flesh is opposed to that, I must continually work to attain to that level of understanding, becoming more and more a child of light and laying aside the darkness from which I was delivered. Paul reminds us to work at it because it does not come naturally, but the rewards are ours as we live in the joy of knowing our Father better.

How do you think we can better know what pleases God?
(*For further study, read Psalm 119.*)

*Father, help me as I seek to know You more, learning
every day to do the things that are pleasing in Your sight.
Forgive me as I fail, but give me strength and
wisdom to continue on in this journey.
Amen.*

63

Letting the Light of Christ Shine!

Ephesians 5:11-14

"Take no part in the unfruitful works of darkness, but instead expose them. For it is shameful even to speak of the things that they do in secret. But when anything is exposed by the light, it becomes visible, for anything that becomes visible is light. Therefore it says, 'Awake, O sleeper, and arise from the dead, and Christ will shine on you.'"

Paul has already said that once we become children of God through the blood of Jesus Christ, we are the light and must no longer walk in darkness. He continues in these next few verses to elaborate on the results of being the light of the world.

Once we live as light in a dark world, our lights shine through the darkness, through the evil deeds that exist outside of Christ, and thereby exposing them. The world will look at us and scratch its collective head, wondering what is up with us and why we are acting so differently. They may condemn us and call us names, but in truth, the light of Christ in our lives will shine so brilliantly on the darkness in which they live that this darkness is exposed. Some will run in the opposite direction, but some will come to the Lord, seeking the very light they once condemned.

In that glorious moment, we can all sing with the saints: "Arise, O sleeper, and arise from the dead, and Christ will shine on you." All to the glory of God!

– Study/Meditation –

How does your life expose the darkness of the world? How can you live more as the light so that others may see its beauty in comparison to the darkness the world has to offer?

*Father, help me to shine in a dark world through Your grace.
May those around me see only You in my actions and reactions. Amen.*

64

For Such a Time as This

Ephesians 5:15-17

*"Look carefully then how you walk, not as unwise but as wise,
making best use of the time, because the days are evil.
Therefore do not be foolish, but understand
what the will of the Lord is."*

It's often easy to get wrapped up in this temporal existence, forgetting to set our eyes on eternity. However, while we are here on this earth, we must also remember that we were set here by God to work for Him. Every day we live now is to be a day that gives glory to our Father and seeks to advance His Kingdom.

With that in mind, we must heed admonitions like the one Paul gives in today's verses to make every moment count for the Lord, allow every word bring honor to Him, and commit every action for His glory. No moments are wasted. After all, just as Mordecai told Esther, how do we know whether or not we were put in this place for such a time as this?

– Study/Meditation –

How is it foolish to waste even a moment of our time here on this earth?
How do we reconcile this truth with the fact that we also live for eternity?

*Father, help me to live my life here on this earth with
You always at my center. Give me the wisdom and discernment
to walk in understanding and not in foolish behavior.
Thank You for guiding me. Amen.*

Filled with the Holy Spirit

Ephesians 5:18-20a

*"And do not get drunk with wine, for that is debauchery,
but be filled with the Spirit, addressing one another in psalms
and hymns and spiritual songs, singing and making melody to the Lord
with all your heart, giving thanks always."*

Although Paul is addressing here a particular pagan custom in the worship of Dionysus, the god of wine, he is saying something very significant for us today. Paul is reminding us that if we fill ourselves with anything that takes the place of the Holy Spirit, such as alcohol or drugs or anything else, we are neglecting who we really are – children of the light.

Paul has been writing over and over in Ephesians that we must behave according to both who we are and Whose we are, not like the world from which we have been removed. Being filled with the Spirit manifests itself in uplifting one another by God's Word, singing to God with all of our hearts, and always giving thanks for what He has given us. If we are living and speaking through the Spirit that now lives in us, there will be no room for anything the world has to offer.

– Study/Meditation –

How can you more behave as a spirit-filled believer?
How does this sort of behavior affect those around you?

*Father, help me to remain free from the influences
of this fallen world around me, instead living as the spirit-filled
believer that I am. Thank You for giving me the Holy Spirit
as my guide in this life. Amen.*

Submission

Ephesians 5:20-22

"Give thanks always and for everything to God the Father in the name of our Lord Jesus Christ, submitting to one another out of reverence for Christ. Wives, submit to your own husbands, as to the Lord."

Even though our focal passage for the next couple of days really begins with verse 22, it is necessary to back up to what Paul says in the last section for contextual understanding. As discussed, Paul has been reminding the Ephesians, and us, about how we are to live so that we are displaying the light that is in us. At this point in his letter, he is speaking of how we should treat one another, submitting to one another and serving one another as unto the Lord. He begins this section with wives but will then speak to all categories of readers, giving more specific direction to each but all with the same goal – submission to God through our treatment of others.

Consequently, he begins this section with encouraging wives to submit to their husbands "as to the Lord." This doesn't mean "as if he is the Lord," as is often misconstrued. What Paul is saying is: "Wives, submit to, or serve your husbands as unto the Lord; serve them and submit to their leadership because of obedience to God's order and God's direction."

I don't submit to my husband because he necessarily deserves it; nor do I do so because he has given me what I think I deserve. I do so as unto Christ. I do so in obedience to my Lord, and in that God is honored. It's no different than why we are to serve others in appropriate ways, referring always back to verse 21: "Submit to one another out of reverence to Christ."

(continued)

66

Submission — continued

– Study/Meditation –

Why are these kinds of verses so highly contested in our society? What truths should we keep at the forefront of our minds so that these kinds of mandates become clearer?

Father, thank You for Your direction so specifically given in Your Word. Help me to lay myself aside and in obedience to You serve others daily. Please forgive me when my pride prohibits me from this obedience.
Amen.

Roles Within Marriage

Ephesians 5:23-24

*"For the husband is the head of the wife even as Christ
is the head of the church, his body, and is himself its Savior.
Now as the church submits to Christ, so also wives should submit
in everything to their husbands."*

Many have often argued that verse 21, when speaking of mutual submission, negates anything in verses 22-24, when speaking of individual submission. However, this is a restricted and incorrect view of what Paul is saying here.

On the one hand, we are all to submit to and serve one another as fellow believers in Christ, but that fact does not preclude the distinctive roles each of us has been given in the Kingdom of God. Furthermore, those roles do not define importance; they simply define roles. God has clearly given man the role of spiritual head of the household, and inasmuch, he bears a spiritual responsibility for that household. Wives are not to give up their identities or their wills when submitting, but they are to recognize their husbands' leadership within the marriage and family.

Perhaps John Piper and Wayne Grudem said it best: "Submission refers to a wife's divine calling to honor and affirm her husband's leadership and help carry it through according to her gifts. It is not an absolute surrender of her will. Rather, we speak of her disposition to yield to her husband's guidance and her inclination to follow his leadership." (Piper, John and Wayne Grudem, Recovering Biblical Manhood and Womanhood, Crossway Books, 1991). If we believe all that the Word says about God's character and purpose, then we must believe that He knows what is best within our marriages, too.

(continued)

Roles Within Marriage – *continued*

– Study/Meditation –

What is the significance of the God-ordained roles for
husbands and wives in terms of Christ being referred to as
the Bridegroom and the church His bride? Why do you think many
women fight against these roles?

*Father, help me to recognize that You have set the
correct order for things because that order works best. Help
me to pleasingly fulfill my role within Your Kingdom, setting
myself aside and placing You first. Forgive me for the
times when I fail at this. Amen.*

68

Christ's Love for the Church

Ephesians 5:25-27

"Husbands, love your wives, as Christ loved the church and gave himself up for her, that he might sanctify her, having cleansed her by the washing of water with the word, so that he might present the church to himself in splendor, without spot or wrinkle or any such thing, that she might be holy and without blemish."

It is truly a grand thing that the relationship most compared in the Bible with Christ's relationship with the church is that between a husband and wife. Paul tells us how in these few verses.

Christ's love for His church, for His Bride, is a sacrificial love. It is not a love that is based on merit, nor is it a love based on her deserving it. Christ's love for the church is a love that is based on the atonement. He gave up His very own life so that He could give her life everlasting in purity and sanctity. He atoned for her. It is that love that Paul says should fashion a husband's love for his wife. God, in His wisdom, made man the head of the household and in that station He also gave man the responsibility for that household. That love, the only kind of love that can succeed in such a calling, must be one that is selfless and beyond human wisdom. It is a love that is based on the atonement.

Yes, it is a grand thing, and outside of Christ, it is an impossible thing. But in Him, it is perfect and it is beautiful.

(continued)

68

Christ's Love for the Church – continued

– Study/Meditation –

What is the difference between the way we love each other and the way Christ loves us? How can we work at attaining Christ's love for each other, especially in our marriages?

Father, thank You for the atoning love of my Bridegroom.
Help me to love the way He has called me to love
and forgive me when I don't.
Amen.

A Supernatural Love

Ephesians 5:28-29

"In the same way husbands should love their wives as their own bodies. He who loves his wife loves himself. For no one ever hated his own flesh, but nourishes and cherishes it, just as Christ does the church."

God never calls us to mundane tasks, but instead He calls us to the extraordinary. It is in this light that husbands should view God's extraordinary call to love their wives. God has not called husbands to love their wives as they can, nor has He called them to love their wives as they have learned. A man cannot stand before God one day and claim an inability to love his wife properly because he didn't have an earthly father who modeled that for him. God tells men to fashion their love for their wives after Christ's love for the church, and this is no human love. This love is supernatural; it is extraordinary.

Paul essentially puts a period on this thought in today's verses by saying this love can only humanly be compared to how one loves himself. Whether or not one considers himself to be self-involved, the truth is that all of us are at our deepest levels. We see life through the lens of ourselves, and thereby we filter circumstances and responses and life through that lens. Paul is saying that one example of humanly loving your wife the way that Christ loves the church is by living life for her, not for yourself. It's by putting her needs and her best interests far before your own. This will never come naturally to anyone, but God calls us to supernatural things, things that can only be accomplished in Him.

(continued)

A Supernatural Love – *continued*

– Study/Meditation –

What examples of this kind of love does Christ show for His church?
How can that be translated into a husband's love for his wife?

Father, thank You for the direction You give us in Your Word.
Help me to follow that direction and to always remember
that it is possible in You.
Amen.

The Truth About Marriage

Ephesians 5:30-32

"We are members of his body. Therefore a man shall leave his father and mother and hold fast to his wife, and the two shall become one flesh. This mystery is profound, and I am saying that it refers to Christ and the church. However, let each one of you love his wife as himself, and let the wife see that she respects her husband."

When John Calvin taught from Ephesians, he reflected on how poorly this doctrine was put into practice as he looked around at the marriages he saw. This was in sixteenth century Geneva! Yet, Calvin would say no different today. Why? It is because we so very often view our marriages in the horizontal, when we should in fact be viewing them in the vertical.

Our marriages are supposed to be the closest human representation of our unions with Jesus Christ. Marriage was intended not so that man and woman could find happiness necessarily in each other, though when done correctly that is one result. No, marriage was intended to mirror our union with our Savior, and therefore marriage should be viewed in terms of Christ, not in terms of self or our partner.

We are all a part of the body of Christ, and the union of part to whole is in one way demonstrated in earthly marriage. If this were our truest perspective, the imperfections in our spouses would pale in comparison to the perfection of our Bridegroom.

(continued)

70

The Truth About Marriage – *continued*

– Study/Meditation –

Meditate on our union with Christ. How can a proper
view of this profound mystery help us in all of our
relationships, not just marriage?

*Father, how glorious and magnificent You are! The mysteries
of Your love and Your ways are too high for me to comprehend,
but I worship You in them! Bless me in my relationships and
help me to correctly mirror all that You have given me.*
Amen.

Honor Due Our Parents

Ephesians 6:1-3

"Children, obey your parents in the Lord, for this is right.
'Honor your father and mother' (this is the first commandment
with a promise), that it may go well with you and that
you may live long in the land."

There is probably not much of an argument from believers that today's society has skewed much of what is correct. In Sweden today it is considered a violation of a child's rights for the parent to discipline him/her in any way. The structure for right and wrong and good and bad has been replaced by what looks best for the individual. Yet we know, as Christians, that God's ways are far better and far more effective for both happy and healthy lifestyles.

Paul's continued exhortation in these next nine verses on submitting to and administering authority demonstrate some of these principles. In verses 1-3 he is speaking to children, telling us that obeying our parents is correct for three reasons: it is right, it is commanded, and it is rewarded. Indeed there are nuances to this, as children are still children whether 3-years-old or 43-years-old, but the premise is still the same – there is an honor both to God and to our parents in obedience and respect given to them.

God's order, just as in a marriage, may be difficult at times, but it is always best. Also like the order in marriage, the child/parent order emulates another heavenly relationship – that of our relationship to our Father. Once again the mirroring principle comes into play and our responsibilities are to obey God as we correctly submit to His order.

(continued)

Honor Due Our Parents – *continued*

– Study/Meditation –

How do children honor and obey their parents at any age?
What about aging parents? How do children honor and obey
parents whom they now take care of?

*Father, You are my Father and I know that I honor You
as I honor my earthly parents. Help me to do so in a way
that is well pleasing to You. Amen.*

Godly Parenting

Ephesians 6:4

"Fathers, do not provoke your children to anger,
but bring them up in the discipline and instruction of the Lord."

Paul has preceded this particular admonition with the instruction for children to honor and obey their parents, so even though this verse begins with an address to fathers, we mustn't assume he isn't speaking to all parents. Parenting was created to be a dual effort from both the father and the mother. However, fathers are being given more direct attention here because they are the spiritual heads of the household and will be held accountable for the spiritual well-being of their families. Inasmuch as this is true, fathers do have an added responsibility in bringing up their children so that they are productive members of the God's family.

Additionally, Paul gives a pointed aspect to his instruction by telling fathers (and parents) not to provoke their children to anger while disciplining them and instructing them in the Lord. Our children need to love God and serve God out of a willingness to do so, and that willingness is greatly learned from us. Anger and ill feelings are not the way to achieve such a goal, though discipline and instruction are. This is a tightrope of parenting skills, but it is the role each of us is given when God blesses us with children.

I used to hear a saying that made me smile: "If parenting gets easy, you're doing it wrong!" Parenting is difficult and the responsibilities are immense, but the rewards are wonderful. As in all things, God will always be the answer to life's difficult challenges; that includes raising our children.

(continued)

Godly Parenting – *continued*

– Study/Meditation –

In what ways can a parent exasperate his/her child
so that church and spiritual matters become laborious?
What kind of advice might you give a parent so
that he/she can follow Paul's instruction?

*Father, thank You for giving me Your Word and Your instructions
to guide my every step in life. Help me to seek you in all things –
in raising my children and in living all of my life.*
Amen.

Submission in the Work Place

Ephesians 6:5-8

""Slaves, obey your earthly masters with fear and trembling, with a sincere heart, as you would Christ, not by the way of eye-service, as people-pleasers, but as servants of Christ, doing the will of God from the heart, rendering service with a good will as to the Lord and not to man, knowing that whatever good anyone does, this he will receive back from the Lord, whether he is a slave or free."

It is important when coming to passages like the one today that we don't get caught up in the historical references so as to miss the spiritual message. The relationship of slave to master in first century Rome was a common and accepted one. Paul's intent is not to make a political or even a moral statement about this relationship. His intent is the same as it has been with the family – do all things as unto Christ. He is telling the slaves who have become Christians to do everything they do as loyal servants of Christ.

In everything we do we represent Christ to the world. Everyone has some sort of earthly boss, so everyone answers to someone about something. Working for that person cannot become a question of station in life; working at anything must be a representation of the excellence of Christ. Paul is calling all of us, both in first century Rome and today, to sincerely do the best we can do at whatever we do because we are representing Christ and our relationship to the King of kings.

(continued)

73

Submission in the Work Place – continued

- Study/Meditation -

Not everyone has a godly or even a moral boss.
How can one carry out Paul's instruction in verses 5-8
with a boss who isn't godly? Why is it important that we do so?

Father, help me to carry out all the tasks in my life
with Christ as my focus. Amen.

Knowing Who the Real Master Is

Ephesians 6:9

*"Masters, do the same to them, and stop your threatening,
knowing that he who is both their Master and yours is in heaven,
and that there is no partiality with him."*

Remember that Paul is covering all aspects of "family" for the Christian in this section, be it earthly, spiritual, or community. He is reminding us that everything we do is to be done with eternity in mind. In first century Rome, slavery was an accepted part of the community, and as with any human institution, the roles had been tainted by human depravity. Here he is addressing those in charge, or the "masters" in his society.

For us he is speaking to any time that we are in charge of others, be it in the workplace or the church or the community. Paul says we are to behave the same as when others are over us, and that is doing all of it with eternity in mind. We will all stand before a Holy Judge and give an accounting of our behavior while on this earth. Paul tells us to always remember that this earth is not the end and that what happens here is not the goal. Live with eternal eyes, not temporary ones, and treating one another appropriately will be a lot easier.

– Study/Meditation –

Why do you think Paul particularly calls God "Master" in this verse?
What is the common denominator in verses 5-9?

*Father, guide my behavior, my steps and my words as I deal with others.
Help me to remember that we are first and foremost Your servants
and that my role is to bring You glory. Forgive me when I fail in this
and help me to do those things that please You. Amen.*

75

Be Strong in the Lord

Ephesians 6:10

"Finally, be strong in the Lord and in the strength of his might."

What a wonderful thing that the Apostle Paul has not given us all of these very important, yet extremely difficult directives without finishing those thoughts with the "how" of doing them. He realizes that calling us to live correctly with and for each other is a high endeavor and one that is fraught with challenges every step of the way. He knows that chances are very good that some of us to whom he has given these mandates have been injured within the context of the very church he's calling us to love, or that some of us have hurt those within the church with our own actions and that those relationships are strained at the onset.

Paul knows this and God knows this; that's why Paul's final words will be on how we can be strong, and that is only in the Lord. Our strength for such things cannot come from ourselves; it must have its source completely and only in God. Be strong in the Lord, brothers and sisters, for only there can we love one another the way we should.

– Study/Meditation –

Why is it that we cannot love the way we should without God?
What is it about our relationship with God that
enables us to love correctly?

Father, thank You for loving me first. In that, I know
that You have given me the perfect example of both how and
why I must seek to love others in You. Amen.

76

Standing Against Satan

Ephesians 6:11

*"Put on the whole armor of God, that you may be able
to stand against the schemes of the devil."*

After having spent most of the book of Ephesians exhorting us to Christ-like behavior, Paul now reminds us that the reason we need God to fight this fight is because Satan wants nothing more than to thwart all of that. Satan hates God and he hates us, and everything he does and thinks and plans is to ruin what God purposes.

Whereas we can never fall back on that old saying, "the devil made me do it," we most certainly need to be mindful that the devil will do everything he can to destroy us. Our only defense against such an adversary is God's strength, not our own, so Paul will now spend the rest of his letter reminding us first of who we are fighting and then how we are to fight him. Put on the armor of God, not the armor of man, so that none of the devil's schemes will undermine God's plan for your life.

– Study/Meditation –

Notice that Paul wrote that we are to stand against the "schemes
of the devil." Why do you think he used this particular phrase?
How should this encourage us in our fight?

*Father, You are holy and just and powerful. You are
the only Lord and the only Judge and the only Victor,
and I thank You for choosing me to receive Your Spirit.
Help me today to recognize the schemes of the enemy
and to fight them in You, never in myself.
Amen.*

The Battle

Ephesians 6:12

*"For we do not wrestle against flesh and blood,
but against the rulers, against the authorities, against the
cosmic powers over this present darkness, against the
spiritual forces of evil in the heavenly places."*

Perspective is everything. The lens out of which we view reality will determine how we behave and react within this world. It is paramount that we know and believe and respond in the true reality, and that reality is much, much more than we perceive with our human eyes.

There is a battle that is being waged for the souls of man every day, and that battle is not against mankind. That battle is a spiritual battle and just as Paul reminds us in today's passage, it is a battle that is being waged in the heavenly realm. It is an eternal battle, not a temporal one. Inasmuch as this is true, we have to take seriously this battle in which we fight, knowing that the only victory is in the Lord.

Paul is going to keep driving home the point of putting on the armor of God, but first he wants us to remember that we must do so because we do not fight against man but against evil itself. As soldiers in this fight, we are of no value without the proper weapons of both defense and offense. Know what is real first. Then the armaments of battle make more sense.

– Study/Meditation –

Paul often uses the analogy of fighting or wrestling against evil.
Why do you think this is such an appropriate analogy?
How are you fighting against evil in your day to day walk?
How can you be more successful in this fight?

*Father, I recognize that the battle being waged is against
more than I see, but I also know that You are ultimately victorious.
Thank You so much for giving me the tools I need in
Your Word to wage this fight. You are glorious and mighty
and just, and I praise You in all things. Amen.*

Stand Firm

Ephesians 6:13

"Therefore take up the whole armor of God, that
you may be able to withstand in the evil day, and
having done all, to stand firm."

In three verses Paul has basically repeated the same thing all three times: we are in a battle with evil and only in God is there victory. What Paul knew and what he expected his audience to know was how God portrayed Himself in the Old Testament, especially in Isaiah. God is a warrior. He fights for His people. He is a warrior who defends us and protects us. In Isaiah the very same imagery is used as Paul is about to use for us – the helmet and the breastplate – but applied to God.

We are being told here that we must not be moved by the devil, that we must stand firm, and that we must do so in battle armament that was forged not by human hands but by God Himself. Just like Peter told us, "Beloved, do not be surprised at the fiery trial when it comes upon you to test you, as though something strange were happening to you." (1 Peter 4:12) Let us instead be ready, armed with God and His Word and His might and His strength, and then let us stand firm in the truth that has set us free.

– Study/Meditation –

Why do you think Paul has chosen to use imagery
for the believer that was used originally for God in the Old Testament?
What comfort can we take from that?

Father, help me to lean on You as my Warrior and King,
knowing that You are victorious and that nothing that comes
against me can prosper. Amen.

The Belt of Truth

Ephesians 6:14a

"Stand therefore, having fastened the belt of truth."

As Paul begins his explanation of the armor of God, he begins with truth, and he uses the belt of the soldier to symbolize this. A Roman soldier's leather belt supported and protected his lower abdomen, fastened his tunic together and held his sword. In short, the soldier's belt was the binding that held all of him intact while in battle.

As with the soldier's belt, without truth nothing else we do will matter. Without truth, all else will fade; it will be lost. As Christians in this spiritual battle against the forces of darkness and evil, we have to have truth be the binding that holds all of our lives together. It is true that commentators struggle with whether or not Paul is speaking of God's truth here or integrity of the heart, but upon closest examination, the latter does not exist in its fullness without the former. All things that amount to anything in eternity must be founded on the truth of God which will produce integrity of heart, and both of these things must be the foundations that hold us up in this battle. We must stand first and foremost with truth holding all else together.

– Study/Meditation –

What is the basic foundation of God's truth? (*Hint: Read John 14:1-6.*)

Father, help me to make Your truth bind all of my life together, giving me the strength and wisdom to fight this fight and to do so in the integrity of Your Word. Amen.

The Breastplate of Righteousness

Ephesians 6:14b

"Stand therefore,…having put on the breastplate of righteousness."

A soldier's breastplate was probably one of the most important parts of his armor in that it protected his most vital organ – his heart. Many of the enemy's arrows were deflected due to a good breastplate during wartime. It is completely unsurprising, then, that Paul uses this piece of armor to name the Christian soldier's protection, the breastplate of righteousness.

Once again, commentators disagree as to which righteousness Paul is referring to, either that perfect imputed righteousness of Christ or the sanctifying righteousness we need to become more Christ-like. And once again, the latter is impossible without the former. We must have our hearts imputed with Christ's righteousness and the protection therein; only then can our hearts be further protected from the enemy's arrows as we grow in sanctifying righteousness in our lives. Without hearts that are protected by Christ as well as our own paths toward being like Him, we would have no hope of standing firm in this battle.

We do stand firm, brothers and sisters, because our hearts have been transformed by our Savior and because we continue in our journeys toward righteous behavior that is worthy of this great gift we have been given.

– Study/Meditation –

What happens at the moment of salvation that ensures the believer has the breastplate of righteousness? How can we continue to wear this breastplate in our daily walks?

Father, thank You for the gift of imputed righteousness.
Help me in my daily walk to be more and more like Christ in my
sanctification so that I can stand firm in this day. Amen.

Gospel Shoes

Ephesians 6:15

*"(Stand firm) and, as shoes for your feet, having put
on the readiness given by the gospel of peace."*

Once again, Paul is using the uniform of the Roman soldier to symbolize the areas of readiness needed for the believer to stand firm in the evil day. A Roman soldier wore a half-boot that was designed so that they had flexibility but could also stand firm in the day of battle. These shoes were specially made to give them maximum usage during the fight.

Likewise, Paul says that if we are to stand firm against the schemes of the evil one, we must do so with shoes made of the gospel of peace. The gospel of Jesus Christ gives us peace with God, and the enemy would like nothing more than to convince us that we are at enmity with Him. This peace given to us in the sacrifice of Christ enables us to not only stand firm in the evil day, living for that future hope of eternity with our Father, but it also enables us to live in peace with our fellow brethren for the very same reasons. Consequently, these truths give us the desire to share this message with others.

"Gospel shoes" help us stand firm in peace with both God and our brothers and sisters while also giving us the ability and desire to share this good news with others. In short, the good news of Christ's atonement for our sins is the foundation upon which we stand, and we do so in peace.

(continued)

81

Gospel Shoes - *continued*

– Study/Meditation –

How does our peace with God ready us to stand against
the devil's schemes? How does this same peace enable you
to seek peace with your brothers and sisters?
How can you improve in this area today?

*Father, help me today to stand on Your truths,
on the gospel of Jesus Christ, promoting and spreading
the peace that surpasses all understanding, no matter
what is going on around me. Amen.*

The Shield of Faith

Ephesians 6:16

*"In all circumstances take up the shield of faith,
with which you can extinguish all the flaming
darts of the evil one."*

The writer of Hebrews tells us in Hebrews 11:1, "Now faith is the assurance of things hoped for, the conviction of things not seen." Then the writer goes on for an entire 40 verses giving example after example of what faith looks like in men and women of the bible.

Upon closer inspection of these examples, we can see one common thread, and that thread is not necessarily what man would call a "good life," at least not in earthly terms. What we see are examples of men and women who truly believed what they professed to believe, and consequently, their lives demonstrated that belief. Only with this kind of belief, this faith, could they or any of us come against the schemes of the devil.

The things happening to you today may seem terrible and out of control. It may seem that no good can come from your circumstances, that certainly God has not orchestrated these horrendous events. Fellow believer, only your faith in the promises of God, in what John Piper calls "future grace," can assure you and comfort you in these trying days. Faith is the shield that protects your heart and your soul from crumbling in the face of adversity. Faith is conviction that God is God and that He is faithful to His promises. Stand firm there.

(continued)

82

The Shield of Faith – *continued*

– Study/Meditation –

How can you demonstrate faith in God's promises today?
What does your day to day faith look like?
(*For further study, read Hebrews 11.*)

*Father, I believe that You are who You've said You are
and that Your promises are true. Help me in my daily
struggle to live out this faith so that I can hear You say,
"Well done, my good and faithful child."
Amen.*

83

The Helmet of Salvation

Ephesians 6:17a
"And take the helmet of salvation...."

Every believer, at some time or another, will question his/her salvation. After all, we know ourselves better than anyone else, besides God, and we know what we are capable of. In that knowledge, it's impossible not to wonder why God would choose us.

The enemy loves nothing more than to capitalize on these doubts, making us fearful and frightened of either losing our salvation or of possibly never having had it at all. Paul tells us in this verse that we have to remember the truth of our salvation as another piece of our armor that enables us to fight off the schemes of the devil. We must know truth. We must remember the promises of God, especially those in terms of His faithfulness to His own. Jesus said in John 6:37, "All that the Father gives me will come to me, and whoever comes to me I will never cast out." Know to whom you belong and stand in that wonderful and eternal truth.

– Study/Meditation –

What can separate us from God if we are born again?
(*Hint: Read Romans 8:31-39.*)

Father, thank You for choosing to love and save me.
Thank You for sending Your Son as a sacrificial atonement
so that I might never doubt that I am Yours. Amen.

84

The Sword of the Spirit

Ephesians 6:17b

"(And take) the sword of the Spirit, which is the word of God."

Every piece of the armor that Paul has symbolically given in this passage has been for defensive use until the end. The last piece he tells us to use against the schemes of the enemy is not only a defensive weapon, but it is also an offensive weapon.

A sword can be used to stave off the blows of the enemy or it can be used to attack him. Our offensive weapon is the Word of God, and it is indeed sharper than any two edged sword. Against God's Word the devil has no recourse. That is precisely why when tempted by Satan, even though Jesus could have vanquished him with one word, He quoted the Word of God. It was an example for you and me to see the power that exists within the words of our Lord. Satan's biggest tool against us is our own sin, and without the Bible's truths to guide us, we are lost to that sin.

Psalm 119:11 says, "Your word I have stored up in my heart, that I might not sin against you." Wield the weapon of weapons. Know the words of God, and the devil's plans will come to no avail.

– Study/Meditation –

Why do you think God's Word is the weapon we must use to offensively fight the devil? How can we use it?

Father, thank You for Your words. Thank You for making them so readily available so that I can fight the schemes of the enemy. You are mighty and Your words are mighty and I praise Your Name. Amen.

The Weapon of Prayer

Ephesians 6:18a

"Praying at all times in the Spirit, with all prayer and supplication."

Paul is giving us the final instruction in our battle against the schemes and plans of the devil, and that is prayer. It is the strongest and most effective tool in our arsenal, and yet we often go to it as a sort of last resort.

Instead, Paul tells us to pray at all times, that is having a continual attitude of prayer, an attitude that recognizes and petitions a living and active God to aid and guide us in every circumstance. He goes on to say that we must pray all kinds of prayers, those of thanksgiving and adoration, as well as those that petition the Lord for help.

When we pray about all things, remembering to also proclaim how great and majestic God is, we are comforted in that acknowledgement, and the devil is simply and totally defeated. Pray at all times, in all ways, and for all things. God is glorified in that and we are comforted.

- Study/Meditation -

How can you pray at all times? What does that look like
in a practical manner? How is prayer our best defense and
offense against the devil?

Father, I praise You in all things and worship You always.
Thank You for what You have given me and for what You have
forgiven me. Guide me in this day and protect me
from the evil one. Amen.

The Battle Line of Prayer

Ephesians 6:18b

*"To that end keep alert with all perseverance,
making supplication for all the saints."*

The phrase that stands out most in this part of verse 18 is "keep alert with all perseverance." In other words, "keep on staying alert," and how do we do that? We do that through prayer. We pray in all things at all times, and we recognize that our prayers are not simply so that God can protect us or bless us. Our prayers should primarily be in response to this great spiritual battle that is ensuing around us at every minute of every day.

In that we also remember that this battle is not one we fight alone; all believers are fellow soldiers in this fight and we must protect one another. We do this in prayer. We fight for one another and protect one another by praying for one another. Paul is reminding us to fight the good fight in a battle line of prayer.

– Study/Meditation –

Why is this visual that Paul creates in Ephesians 6 so effective?
How can you improve your "good fight" today?

*Father, please protect and bless my fellow brothers and sisters,
both those that I know and those that I don't. Protect those
in the mission field and give them victory in their spiritual
and physical endeavors. Amen.*

Asking for Prayer

Ephesians 6:19

"And (pray) also for me, that words may be given to me in opening my mouth boldly to proclaim the mystery of the gospel."

We shouldn't pass over the importance of what the Apostle Paul is asking of his congregation in these verses. This is the Apostle Paul, the man who saw the Lord Jesus Christ on the road to Damascus, who was called personally by Him to preach His word. This man is petitioning the Ephesian church to pray on his behalf. If Paul recognized his need for the prayers of his congregation so that he can boldly proclaim the gospel, then we should recognize the need of all ministers for the same from us.

Prayer knits our hearts together, and when we pray for the men and women who diligently teach and preach God's Word, we knit our hearts to theirs. We covenant with them each and every time that we will partner with them in upholding the truth of God's Word. We express before God each time we lift our ministers up in prayer that we understand the gravity and importance of the preaching of His Word.

On Sunday, as many of us prepare to go to our local churches in worship, let us pray for our ministers and teachers that they may boldly and accurately and with courage bring us the very truth of our Lord.

(continued)

Asking for Prayer - *continued*

– Study/Meditation –

Meditate today on how you can more adequately and lovingly
lift up your ministers in prayer. Covenant to do so in response
to this plea from Paul.

*Father, thank You for the men and women You have called
to preach and teach Your word. I pray specifically for my
pastor and ministers that You will bless and protect them, giving
them wisdom in the words that they speak and boldness in
the manner in which they speak them.*
Amen.

Boldly Declaring the Gospel

Ephesians 6:20

""(The mystery of the gospel), for which I am an ambassador in chains, that I may declare it boldly, as I ought to speak."

Paul reminds the Ephesians here of some of the trials he has endured on behalf of this gospel he proclaims, once again using himself as an example of how a believer should live as unto Christ. Paul says he is in chains for the gospel, and then he says he is in chains so that he can keep declaring its truth. That's a mighty statement and one we should take note of.

In a world where often Christians are far more interested in being politically correct than in speaking the truth, it would do all of us a tremendous amount of good to pay attention to Paul's example. Instead of looking for a way out of speaking the truth because it might make us less popular, we should be taking those opportunities to tell of God's Word, speaking it boldly precisely because of the discomfort. After all, the Apostle Paul would tell us that truth is exactly why we are persecuted and that the persecution is exactly why we should tell the truth. This is a great and awesome paradox and one we should be proud to be a part of.

– Study/Meditation –

What might Paul say to the Christian community today in regards to how we must handle certain "politically incorrect" issues we see recently in the news? How can you stand for truth in your community?

Father, help me to be bold for Your truth, caring not for my reputation but only for Your glory. Give me the wisdom to say and do the things that bring honor to Your name. Amen.

Part of a Family

Ephesians 6:21-22

*"So that you also may know how I am and what I am doing,
Tychicus the beloved brother and faithful minister in the Lord will tell
you everything. I have sent him to you for this very purpose, that you
may know how we are, and that he may encourage your hearts."*

Tychicus was the scribe and traveling companion to Paul. He was taking down the dictation of this letter to the Ephesians, and then Paul sent him back to Ephesus to both deliver the letter and then report how they were doing. This is so practical and yet so indicative of how we are to be in the family of believers.

Paul knew that his fellow brethren would want to know how his health was and how the ministry was going. It's the same reason we call our parents or children or friends from time to time – we want to stay in touch. We care about one another and we feel closer to one another when we know what is going on in each other's lives. It is the same within the body of Christ, if not more so. We need reports from our missionaries and our fellow workers from the church; it makes us more of a family and we are comforted in this kind of intimate knowledge. We are a family. We should care about one another as a family should. Communication, as demonstrated by Paul over and over again, is vital to this relationship.

– Study/Meditation –

What can you do today that will make you more in touch
with your Christian family? Why is this so important?

*Father, thank You for my family. Thank You for Your gracious
and loving mercy in connecting us together through You. I pray for my family,
both for those I know personally and those I do not. Bless them and keep
them in Your loving protection and might. Amen.*

Prayer for Peace

Ephesians 6:23

"Peace be to the brothers, and love with faith, from God the Father and the Lord Jesus Christ."

Paul is closing his letter now with a benediction, or a blessing, and his blessing has two parts.

The first part is in verse 23 as he prays peace, love and faith for them. First he is praying that the brethren have peace. He is speaking of this in a two-fold manner, as all of us must when praying that we have peace. He is praying that they live in peace with each other as the family of God, but more importantly that they live in the peace they have in knowing they are part of the family of God. We most certainly should be a people of peace in our lives with the knowledge that we have been given eternal life in perfection with our Lord. There is great peace in that, and God's children should live within that peace.

Then Paul prays also that we would live in the love of God which we receive by faith in Him. Truly the peace he has prayed over us is only possible when we know the love that has been given to us by God, and we know that love by faith. Peace, love, and faith: Paul very aptly begins his blessing with these and it is in these that all of us can and should live as the family of God.

– Study/Meditation –

Most biblical benedictions begin as "grace and peace," but Paul begins his as "peace and grace." In light of the rest of this letter, why do you think his blessing is stated this way? (*Hint: What was the purpose of the letter to the Ephesians?*)

Father, thank You for the peace that only You can give. I praise You in Your glory and honor You in that peace. I love You. Amen.

lovetruthlive

WITH DEB WATERBURY

Teaching that the love of Christ
and the Truth of Scripture lead
to life-changing freedom

*"By this all people will
know that you are my
disciples, if you have
love for one another."*
– John 13:35

debwaterbury.com

lovetruthlive

WITH DEB WATERBURY

PAINTED WINDOW TRILOGY:
Painted Window, Threads and White Zephyr

Follow Elizabeth Percy's allegorical
journey into discovering the love
that transforms all of our lives –
the love of Jesus, our Bridegroom.

James on the Mount

A study of the book of James as it relates
to the Sermon on the Mount.

DAILY DEVOTIONAL SERIES:

Bible devotional studies, verse by verse.

- *Galatians* (3 month devotional)
- *Ephesians* (3 month devotional)
- *Philippians* (3 month devotional)

WOMEN'S MINISTRY STUDIES:

6 Pairs of Sandals
Yesterday's Footsteps and Today's
Women's Ministry

ADDITIONAL RESOURCES AT

www.debwaterbury.com

Dr. Deb Waterbury
also offers:
Windows of the Heart Podcast Teachings
(also available through iTunes)
and
Voices of Love Blogs

Visit us on Facebook, Twitter, Instagram,
LinkedIn, Pinterest and YouTube

Note:
*Dr. Deb Waterbury continues to expand
her resource catalogue, so please log onto
her website for the most recent additions.*

Made in the USA
Columbia, SC
30 August 2018